Acknowledgments

Dedicated to anyone that has ever
felt the hollowness of abuse.
You are not alone. Never let the darkness win.

Thank you to my greatest supporter, my love, Michael.
Without your loving acceptance, I couldn't do this.
Your love is infinite. I wish you could see it within yourself.

THE YOWLING MOON
Breathes blistering light
Into the vale of the night.
Burying bodies in the garden
Veins have withered and died; Like
Wilting orchids on the vine
Clinging to the tree of life,
Calloused and forgotten
Into the weight of the night

Do you believe in monsters?

If I could tell you there's no such thing as monsters, believe me, I would. But I would only be lying to you.

I've always been drawn to the truth. That being said, the truth isn't all it's cracked up to be. Honesty, to me, is more meaningful than any beautifully gilded lie. Even if the lie is meant to spare offense. I prefer the truth above all else, especially when it's hard to swallow.

I find the diamonds in between the lines of the lies of what other people would rather say.

History and all of its tales are filled with white lies bordering absolute bullshit. History is falsified to hide the inhumane savagery, to make who the storytellers and governing bodies want you to like as the hero.

Personally, I don't want the cleaned-up version anyone could read. What fascinates me is the ugly truth. My personal distortion is when I find something to be true, even if no one else agrees, I can not be swayed from my judgment.

I admit that I am judgemental, but I also have no desire to judge anyone, not for any other reason than to expand my own perception. My opinions don't really matter, even if or when they make the most sense. The world doesn't actually make sense. It's a realization that is difficult to initially digest. But here's the thing...

A savage exists in every living thing. It's the animal inside. The only difference between animals and humans is the ability to choose control. We are taught the concept of right and wrong, unlike other creatures.

A savage and disease only differ because the savage can choose whether or not to do harm. An illness can not stop. It does not decide to pause even when it lays dormant. It has no mind. It's only waiting for the right conditions to strike. It's only a matter of time.

A parasite does not hibernate the same way a disease does. It devours until there's nothing left to destroy, or the body finds a way to exterminate it. An illness is invisible, often left undetected until it leaves the body distressed or debilitated. Sometimes even then, the cause remains unknown.

What makes a shadow incapable of harboring disease? The shadow lies behind your door, crawling underneath your bed. Creatures of darkness stalk you in your bedroom to surround you when you should feel the safest. Its agenda is simply to feed upon your deepest fears and infest your dreams.

The hollowness you feel upon awakening is the stolen dreams you'll never comprehend. Dreams are replaced with nightmares or, at the least, the feeling of living through horror. Going to sleep again becomes more impossible with each passing day.

The darkness is now feeding on you as you torture yourself, fearing ever going to sleep again.
The slithering underneath your skin, which feels like insects begging for release, is only a sign that the demon likes you.
Uncomfortable irritability is the residue of being haunted by the unseen.
The darkness must have you.

There's another world that the living can not enter, covered in the inescapable tar of obsidian shadow. The entrance to the dark world is nonexistent, even though the shadow may come and go as it pleases. It corrupts the mind, incites irrational fear, and feeds on pain and sorrow whenever it gets hungry. The monsters of the darker world can lead a human parasite to your door. It already has control of their mind. It's a plague that feeds upon every negative thought of each victim it has chosen. It's a burden and a curse that must be carried silently. The veil between this world and theirs is much too thin; it's maddening. Believing only causes disbelief. Being possessed by it can not be trusted or foreseen.

Monsters are a creation curated for children to develop a sense of fear without giving them an object to place it on. It's a necessary evil, helping their survival in an unknown world one strange thought at a time. Nobody is born understanding the dangers of the world. Threats of harm are the only way children will survive. Fire will burn, water can drown, and the streets are filled with cars driving too fast to slow down. Threats of death and destruction are the only way to stay alive. An abundance of necessary fear is given to a child, and naming them all is an endless task. Giving them a monster to fear with unknown agendas and desires is the fastest way to sum up everything that could possibly cause them harm.

The divide where necessary fear resides and preferences without consequence meet is a thin line that often gets misplaced. Is any superstition being passed down as the truth instead of personal judgment? This is where fear becomes evil, creating violence and disorder. Animosity is the most destructive force on Earth, aside from mass panic. All the ... isms and phobias are based upon fear that has transformed into loathing. The economy wouldn't thrive as well without the construct of fear.

Why would you need security systems, fencing, locks, guns, or any self-defense items? It's because you never know where, when, or how the monster will strike. The children are no longer safe, not even in school. There are shootings, illnesses, guns brought in, and bullies that create a mind filled with endless torment.

No place is safe unless you know that you are never safe. We live in a society, but it's more like a war zone. *Don't cower down. Just be aware. The only thing you have to fear is fear itself.*

It's essential to begin the fear process as casually as possible, in a non-threatening way. Instead of saying goodnight, let's say, "Sleep tight and don't let the bedbugs bite." It's a well-known phrase intended to translate to, 'sleep well with pleasant dreams.' *How did it get confused?*

It got lost in translation somehow when beds were initially hoisted above the ground with chains to keep them from touching the floor for cleanliness. However, it invokes a sense of danger even when said jestingly. Children don't know what exists within the world. What's to keep a bed bug from being seen, yet not something make-believe? In fact, a bed bug is an insect that feasts bountifully on your blood as you sleep, crawling from the edge of the bed or under a fitted sheet, and it can wait, under the right circumstances, as long as a year to feed. Whatever may be imagined is not quite as bad as their actual appearance or the feeling of the moist burst of liquid when you smash one sucking the blood from your slumbering body. It's fabled that you can not feel them feeding. Maybe some people can't. Their bite is not quite as bad as the feeling of their fast-moving spiny legs carrying the weight of your blood in their fully engorged bodies. It's enough to give anyone nightmares.

Any fear can become a monster, an obsession that takes any form. This terror occurs before you even close your eyes to sleep.

Innocence is fragile. What is taught to the children is how they will flourish, much like a plant. Give it the right amount of water, sun, shade, and oxygen, and the plant will thrive. How do we teach acceptance without teaching loss? How do we stay safe without knowing fear? The world is terrifying. As long as the children are raised with love, it will shine through as bright as the sun. The darkness cannot survive in the light.
If given the opposite, even if your plant grows, the void is all that will feel like home. This is where the monsters thrive.

Welcome to my mind.

I can't promise it will all make sense, but it's ominous and intense. I want to tell you the story of my life. It's the only proof I have of the darkness, the human parasite, and all of the demons that thrive from the other world that most people can not see. I could tell you a story about all the well-known psychopaths and killers, but my monsters aren't famous. I can't speak for what darkness caused their destruction and consumption of life. I could only assume like anyone else. My monsters are not widely known, and I'd like to bring them out into the light. Few people would think that a demon could be sitting beside them. If it comes to mind, the observation is often corrupted by personal judgment. You would be surprised by how many monsters appear to look completely normal. Evil can take any form. Irrational fear and necessary fear are difficult to separate once combined. The shadows do not make themselves known until you can't help but know that they're standing in front of you.

1. Mama and the sky

My discovery of monsters began with my father. His appearance was indistinguishable from the Beast, from 'Beauty and the Beast.' He stood as tall as the top of a door and was rather husky. His hair formed more of a mane around his face, composed of a dark shoulder-length mullet with curls at the ends, prominent sideburns, and a horseshoe mustache. His peridot green eyes glowed like fire, and you felt the burn staring through you when he was enraged and looking at you. He was often absent from home, as his days were spent working as an Over-The-Road truck driver, hauling items across the country until his workload was through. Sometimes instead of coming home, he'd work another truckload to be on the road longer. Nobody knew when he was coming back home, if ever.

As a three-year-old girl, it seemed like he was gone for months. The intervals between work and home are lost on me because of this. Sometimes I forgot that I had a father. Forgetting was the dream.

I spent every moment with Mom, my beautiful glowing angel with the most intricate cerulean blue eyes. Her skin was like white sand softened by the sea. Her voice was one with the wind, kind, gentle, containing a song you never want to end. It's the sound of the sea in a seashell; if only an angel was the sea.

Our days together consisted of walking to the park that was just across the street from the small apartment where we resided. I would play at the park as Mom watched me, spending as long as I liked climbing, sliding, and being pushed on the swing. Sometimes she would let me sit in her lap on one of the swings, 'spider style' as she called it. I would sit on her lap with my head on her chest, listening to her heart as the breeze brushed the back of my neck as we swung out. I was carried by an angel in flight as she held me.

Mom and I often visited the library afterward, just a few minutes from the park. The path led through half a mile of grassy hills, down sidewalks with drainage pipes underneath their cement pathways, until reaching a green-painted bridge with wooden planks to walk upon leading to the library doors. It never felt very far as I held Mom's hand and watched the tiny grass hills under my feet appear and plummet underneath our steps in soft and steady waves. At the library, we would look for books to read before bed.

Bill Peet was my favorite author, writing unique and exciting stories with creative illustrations that boggled my mind. Occasionally we'd stay for story time or a puppet show to give Mom time to discover books to read on her own.

We'd watch movies on the couch together at home, cuddling with our two cats, Tommy and Jerry.
Tommy was Mom's soft gray tabby cat with black vertical bands scattered across his body like an abstract painting. Jerry was the orange version of Tommy, my playful tiger.
Sometimes I would get Jerry to dance with me. I would hold his paws in my hands and stand him up to be as tall as I was. He was the perfect dance partner. I would let him go if he pulled away, but Mom told me it was cruel of me to force him to dance. Eventually, I stopped trying to make him dance if I was really being mean.
Once, I found him standing on two feet with his hands out, dancing a dizzy circle by himself.
I exclaimed, "Look, he dancing!"
He fell back to the floor and began walking on four legs.
"Cats just aren't meant to do that, sweetie," Mom said.
I was disappointed that she couldn't see how adorable Jerry was as he enjoyed a dance of his own.

In all our time alone together, I only once saw Mom cry. I discovered her face down on her bed, silently spilling steady tears. Without seeing her face, I knew something was wrong.

The room was dark, and the color around her was dim like her bright aura had been extinguished somehow. She could light up a room simply by walking into it on any typical day as long as my father wasn't home.

Walking in slowly, as a trespasser, I whispered, "Mama okay?"

She responded with illegible sobs, "...they're gonna.. take you away. They'll ask if I'm a good mom, and they'll take you away. I don't know what I'm doing anymore." Her tears fell harder, faster, plummeting from her face like a heavy downpour.
I stuttered, "Who, Mama? Who taka me fom wu? I say go away!"
She laughed between her sobs, "No baby, you can't say that. It's rude."
I scoffed, "I say it, and dey go away. I dun care if ruude. I'm not ruude, dey rue! Is my Mama!"
The light around her brightened as she smiled. Tears stained her face from before, but they no longer fell from her eyes.
Her hand brushed against my face softly as she whispered, "Do you really mean that?"
I nodded excitedly as I continued, trying to cheer her up, "Yes, I tell dem. We goto par..."
She began sobbing again, "No baby, we can't go to the park. They're coming to ask you things, things about Mama. To see if Mama is good at being Mama. I just... I don't think I'll ever be good enough. It's never enough." Mom kept upsetting herself more while I was trying to cheer her up. I was getting a bit frustrated now.
I exasperated, "No Mama, we no go ri now. I know! We alway go. We go yesteray, we go tomowwow, all a time. Nobody say you bad. Always good. Mama is a bes Mama in da whole wie worl."
She wiped the tears from her face as she lit up with pride. She was no longer afraid of the evil men coming. CPS was coming to investigate our house upon an anonymous complaint that stated I was being neglected. It was the furthest thing from the truth.

Mom let the case worker in when he came knocking. He

was a short fellow with dark hair and wore a suit and tie. I thought about asking why he wore a suit, but I changed my mind.

Mom tried to speak to him, but he declined, saying, "I'd just like to talk to her alone if you don't mind. I want to see how she's doing without pressure to answer any certain way. I'll leave the door open so you can observe the conversation. It shouldn't take long."

She hesitantly consented as he walked where I sat on the bed watching television. He sat directly in front of the screen. I felt instantly annoyed by him, as he just *had* to show up when *Alladin* was being shown. I had seen it countless times but could never get enough of Genie. The man in the suit asked, "How are you?"

I huffed, "I be better if I coud watch 'ladin."

He looked behind him at the screen and moved over, realizing he was in the way.

I smiled, "tank you."

He smiled back, "You're very welcome, Miss... what name do you go by?"

I was already annoyed by his questions. I replied, "I Annie."

I returned to watching Aladdin as the carpet had just shown up, dancing around, pestering Abu. I zoned out for a moment until the man in the suit moved to where he had initially sat to get my attention away from the TV.

I sighed, "Wha you say?"

He asked, "What does an average day look like? Do you spend time with your mom, go anywhere, and have fun? I see you like to watch cartoons. You look very healthy."

I wasn't sure what healthy meant, but I answered, "Mama taka me to a park. We wal to libarry, she swing me, and stuff like dat."

He nodded and smiled as he listened. He continued, "Good. That sounds like a lot of fun. What else can you tell me... Tell me about Mama. Is she a good mom? How does she take care of you?"

I replied, "Mama is a bes mama in da 'ole wie worl. We watcha movie togeder, she taka me eberywere. Is only love. I love a you, Mama!"

Mom replied in tears, "I love you too, baby."

The man in the suit nodded and stood up.

Lastly, he stated, "You seem very happy here. I can tell you live in a place filled with love. I'll let you get back to your show and won't bother you anymore."

He walked to where Mom stood in the kitchen with her hands on the counter. He shook her hand and nodded at her, saying words I couldn't hear over Genie singing. I watched her smile as he began walking out the door. She locked the door behind him and came over to me in her bed.

She smiled as she rubbed my back, "You did a great job, baby girl. I'm proud of you. Nobody is taking you away because you answered so well, like a big, big girl."

I sat up and leaned against Mom, hugging her tightly in my arms. I told her she was the best mom in the entire world and went back to watching Aladdin, knowing Mom wouldn't be sad about this anymore. The case was dismissed without another word.

The child protection agency is not a monster. An idea can be as destructive as any force on Earth. An idea can turn into a dark obsession that spins out of control. Anxiety is a monster. Fear resides in the belief that one person in a government body can have the power to remove a child from an unfit home without the definition of what that really means.

Are you a bad parent because you're poor, busy, or too worn out to do everything you'd like to be able to do with your child? You're not.

Being a parent is mentally and physically draining, especially when your role is threatened. Someone will judge you regardless of what you do because it's not what they do personally. Strangers do not care to see your perspective. There are too many assumptions and judgments being thrown at parents. It is a job with constant scrutiny from at least one person at all times. It's often a thankless job.

If someone has a problem with you, they'll call CPS to see if they can take your child away from you to annihilate your world. This idea is devastating if you truly love your kids. Humans are often cruel.

Sometimes a child does need to be saved by the child protection agency. Kids are neglected, abused, starved, and treated worse than garbage, somewhere every day, closer than you might expect. They are caged like animals, fed nothing but fear and torment. Someone needs to save them. Not all children can be saved. It's not as easy as you might think to spot. CPS is needed to locate them. Complaints are followed because there is no other way to find them. Sadly, most complaints are not about the children where the nightmares happen. Those kids are left in the dark with no way to find them, although they typically are found eventually due to honest, well-meaning tips given to the agency to suspicious families.

Always remember that you are enough if you're trying your best. If even all you have to give some days is ten percent, then you are giving one hundred percent of all you have. If you have love, care, and want to make them smile every chance you get... Never doubt that you are not enough because you are perfect for them. All a child needs is love and encouragement.

When Dad returned home from his work trips, life was completely different.

He treated Mom like a possession instead of the perfect being she was. The glowing angel seemed to fly away, leaving only the outer shell of Mom. All she wanted was to was find her soul that had flown away as soon as Dad entered our home.

Dad was constantly trapping her in, arguing with her over anything possible. I witnessed every disagreement in the small apartment that only seemed minuscule when he was there. In most disagreements, Mom would head for the front door in the heat of an argument to try to get some air and collect her thoughts. Dad would never allow her to take a break outside. Instead, he'd rush to the door behind her and slam it shut so she couldn't escape.

He'd laugh, "Where do you think you're going anyway? You don't have any friends."

Her response was never the same, consisting of random places or cleverly barking, "to go fuck your mother," or "to hell where you came from."

It was a constant reenactment as if it were some predictable soap opera called The Angel and the Beast. It wasn't a very good show.

She locked herself in the bathroom once, but he took his time and removed the handle from the door as she cried, "No, Go away. Please go away. Leave me alone. I just want to use the bathroom."

Dad laughed sinisterly. It was all just a sick game to him. Dad loved making her feel powerless with nowhere to go. He loved her with negging contempt, constantly reminding her there was no escape and nobody would want her there even if she could get away.

Watching them filled me with a heavy-hearted sense of abandonment. She wasn't just trying to leave him. I was there too. She seemed to forget that I existed when Dad was around. His drama took over our world, and her hopelessness took away the best things about her. It's impossible to be yourself when the person you're with constantly calls you undesirable and makes you feel powerless but somehow still wants you all for themselves like it's a noble cause or a favor being done on the victim's behalf.

Trips to the park were non-existent, bedtime stories were left to my imagination, and libraries were a myth my mind made up. Our only escape was out on the balcony at night, staring out against the black sea of stars.

There was something empirical about the dark diamond sky, more fascinating than even a never-ending universe and more powerful than anyone could ever know.

Every night, I searched for the star that would wink at me after discovering it accidentally. I called it mine. I was curious to know if the star had chosen me or if I had chosen it. All I knew was it spoke to me in a voice devoid of language, only feeling the connection, communicating telepathically, and reverberating deeply as if it held my heart in its grasp.

The feeling was overwhelming yet incredibly soothing.

My star resonated, "Hello, little one. How can I help you? How do you define happiness?"

I answered silently, "I wish... I just want someone to save Mama. To take us away. Dad makes her sad. She isn't the same when he's around. Make sure Mama takes me with her, please. Give her a knight in shining armor to save us from Dad, tell her she's beautiful, and show her just how amazing she really is. Show her what true love is because Mama doesn't know. I want nothing more than for her to be happy and for there to be no more fights. For her light to always be as bright as you are. You're the brightest star, the only one I see. You're my mama of the sky."

My star winked, translating to a giggle to my compliment, "I'll see what I can do. I can't make any promises."

I looked down with a stomach-churning feeling of disappointment. Mom would leave me and run away, but at least she would be happy. That must be what my star meant.

I raised my head back up and stared at the star once more as it faded. I whispered, "That's okay."

Mom asked as she stood beside me, "What'd you say, baby?"

Realizing I had spoken the last words aloud, I clarified, "Is gonna be okay, is all."

Mom sighed hopelessly, "I hope so, baby girl. I hope so."

My star faded away into the dark sky, and I went back inside without having to be led to bed. I would set Mom free, reluctantly, if only she would be happier. Conflicted between acceptance and melancholy, I forced myself to sleep.

I found a second religion out there, staring at the stars.

Nobody knew I wasn't making childish wishes.

I didn't know at first, but I was talking to the goddess of the sky in her glittering dress. I wonder if Mom was making wishes on the stars when she stood next to me. Did she find her piece of heaven in the sky? Or was she thinking how afar she would soar if she could fly? Sometimes it felt like she was already as far away as any ball of light in the sky. I wondered if she made the same wish, just without me in it.

Mom was too young to be a mother, being only sixteen when I was born, and thrown into the chaotic world of being a single mother. Is it better or worse, expecting to parent all on your own? Being with the wrong person can make you feel more alone than you could ever feel actually being alone. Any sense of previous happiness gets expunged, leaving nothing but a black hole inside your heart, slicing into your soul like a cheese grater, slowly shaving away all the beautiful parts, and leaving nothing but the carcass of what used to shine so vibrantly.

Nevermore.

The wrong person can cause your mind to eat away itself like a tape-worm that can't stop feeding. It's arduous trying to focus well enough to even enjoy the bliss of motherhood and being loved by your child when a beast is making you loathe everything about yourself, for everything you do, and for even being alive. It was like he wanted her to fail, to crash and burn until she felt she couldn't do anything alone and would need him to rescue her. She was more independent than that. She bloomed in his absence.

Dad assumed Mom's unhappiness occurred because he was rarely home, so he quit his job as a trucker and began working at *Waffle House* as a cook. He was making less money by changing jobs, so Mom had to find a job as well.

Mom began working at a cable company making sales calls and seemed to enjoy the work. Initially, my parents began to quarrel less often. Mom didn't try to escape anymore, and Dad didn't argue as much as he did before.

We moved into a trailer down the street from my

grandparents so they could watch me while my parents went to work. The trailer park was out in the country, surrounded by pastoral greenery, inhabited by an occasional cow. Mostly, it was just a hilly countryside surrounded by fences and randomly placed homes that seemed miles away from one another until reaching the trailer park. At the beginning of the trailer park stood a beer and wine store, which seemed to be the perfect place as there were no other stores for miles, although there were never any cars sitting in its parking lot. The store seemed abandoned until Papa took me to get beer and cigarettes when he ran out once. The store was much smaller than its outside appeared. There had to have either been a bar or a game room in the back that I never got to see. Either way, Papa alone had to have kept the little store in business as he drank a case of Coors daily. The employees even knew him by name.

2. The Void

Granny had an extensive bookcase that took over an entire wall. It was filled with an ever-growing supply of VHS tapes arranged alphabetically. The only tapes not in pristine order were a sizable sum of animated films, sectioned in the center of the bookcase for easy access. I spent most of my time picking different movies to watch and enjoying them from the playroom next to the living room, which was full of toy bins. I was often more drawn to the fabric in the room since the playroom doubled as Granny's sewing room.

When Granny discovered me using scraps of cloth to make dresses for *Barbie* dolls, she taught me how to sew by hand. Occasionally she would sew on her sewing machine in the living room as I made tiny dresses on the couch next to her. She enjoyed watching *Charmed* during the evenings, and I was happy to watch with her, especially since she rarely left the kitchen.

Granny routinely spent her days sitting in a black cushioned metal chair in the kitchen while appearing rather melancholy as if the weight of the world rested on the fragility of her shoulders. The stress of such an undertaking caused her to slouch in her chair with her head in her hands. A ceaseless sadness had enrooted itself within her, with no one knowing how to take her gloominess away.

Depression is like a cocoon. It suffocates, paralyzes, and extracts the color out of life, so joy is unattainable. It's a poison of the mind. It often makes it impossible to simply rise from bed on any given day. How Granny found strength was nothing short of courageous.

On no occasion had I ever looked into her dark olive-green

eyes and asked her what was wrong. With the gray smoke of an aura heedlessly revolving around her, I wondered how I could cheer her up. Before I could ask, Mom gave me the answer as if she knew the question would be asked before long.

She said, "You know, your Papa... he wasn't always the man you know now. Granny seems sad because she is sad. She's sad because of what your Papa did to her. Before I was born, Daddy was a bad man. He'd take a wooden board and beat your uncle with it. He'd throw Granny down onto the floor and wouldn't stop beating her with his fists. She waited her whole life to marry that man, and it all went to hell once she did. He was the worst thing that ever happened to her. He never did it to me, which I'm grateful for. He had mostly stopped by then, or I was too little to remember. I was told the stories by your uncle, and when I asked Mom, your Granny, about it, she confirmed that's what happened. That man can not hold his whiskey. Your Granny was the most beautiful bride. See?"

Mom picked up a large white wedding album from one of Granny's drawers in the living room hall. Granny's wedding album was the most beautiful book I had ever seen, covered intricately with lace that was taken from a piece of her wedding dress. The lace laid upon a soft bright, satin cover that had to have been as white as it was on the day it was crafted. It was immaculate. Granny had indeed been the most astonishing bride. She could've been on the cover of any bridal magazine with her million-dollar smile. It lit up the room, even in the black and white photographs. Her joy exuberated so vibrantly, standing at the altar next to a young Papa, as she listened and repeated the vows spoken. I imagined her exclaiming jubilantly, "I do!" She was a vision in her tight lace gown, hugging her dainty frame.

She was like a butterfly; only her metamorphosis was done in reverse. Instead of her wedding day leading to her best life, the best day of her life transitioned into a savage nightmare, trapping her inside an overdeveloped cocoon.

When my grandparents were first married, they lived by

the ocean in a house supported by stilts. I was told it was a beautiful home, overlooking the ocean at every window as if it sat upon its own private island. Their beautiful home collapsed when a destructive hurricane hit their home, causing it to collapse into the ocean. They had come to visit their families when the warning of the hurricane was announced and went back to see if there was anything salvageable. Strangely, the wedding album and a few sets of clothes sat within the rubble where their home had once stood. They moved to Denton to be closer to their parents in the trailer they have lived in since the decimation of their home. It was supposed to be a temporary adjustment until something better could be afforded, but that day never came.

Papa ran an automotive shop from home, and the business fell short of what he thought it would be. The only people needing work were individuals who lived in or had car trouble near the trailer park. His income kept the lights on and food on the table, but nothing further was accomplished.

I imagine she was trying to discover in her mind each day a way to forgive Papa. Divorce was not an option as it was against custom, religion, and the vows promised. *Till death do us part.* Each day the question remained, revolving like a hurricane within Granny's mind. How do you forgive a monster?

Can abuse be dismissed, and if so, when? Is it after so many years of it not happening or after they say they're sorry?

Has Papa ever said sorry without repeating the abuse? Is it even possible to let it go as if it never happened? It had occurred so often that it was impossible to forgive.

He hadn't changed. He had just gotten older.

After a bottle of whiskey, sometimes he felt young again.

Maybe if he went to church with her even once, as she went every Wednesday night and Sunday morning. Perhaps if he asked God for forgiveness, she could also forgive him. It could've been an excellent first step, anyway. She did the best she could, living in the same home where the abuse occurred, sleeping in the same bed with a man that could dare lay a hand on her and her sons in anger. Some days he'd come into the kitchen to wash his hands in the sink, the entire time muttering complaints of all the things he noticed she didn't do, like washing the dirty dishes or sweeping the dusty floors. Depression was inevitable, as it was impossible to forgive the monster my papa had been.

Strangely, Papa was the best man that I had ever known. Someone that has monstrous attributes does not make them solely a monster. Everyone is more than what they appear to be, more profound than the black-and-white abstaining full sight to see. The human mind is full of complexities.

His smile lit up the room like the blinding flash of a camera in the dark. His natural aroma was the musk of soured beer and stale cigarettes. His blue eyes glistened vibrantly, even when I did annoying things like play with the loose hanging skin around his neck that reminded me of a turkey; soft, jiggly, and composed of so many dips and folds.

I felt safe when he was near, like nothing in the world could ever harm me.

I began Kindergarten, so less of my time was spent with Granny.
The year before, I couldn't wait to begin school and see where the yellow bus that picked up children off the side of the road went. The kids always returned for another trip the next morning, so it must have been somewhere interesting. At first, spending the day in a classroom with other people my age was exciting, but the initial enthusiasm soon wore off.

Nap time was the most boring waste of time imaginable, as I spent what felt like hours staring at the ceiling on an uncomfortable blue mat. I couldn't sleep like everyone else, but it didn't exempt me from the time. I had to lie down and be silent on the plastic wrinkled mat on the floor. I often got in trouble for talking to someone else who was awake or sighing too loud, so I'd have to change my color on the door chart. One day I even had to change it to purple.

I cried, " I don't wanna go to a principal's office. I didn't do nothin' wrong. I don't want purple!"

My teacher laughed, "I never send anyone to the principal unless they've been really bad. Although, you'll have to learn to stay quiet during nap time."

The best part of the day was the computer lab, playing math and racing games with my classmates when they played the same game simultaneously. Recess was fun sometimes, but at other times the older kids would push me out of the way.

Once a little girl snorted, "You're tiny. Where's your mommy, little girl? You don't know where she is? You need to go tell her this is a school, not a playground! Go play somewhere else instead."

The children in my class were kind, but the other kids always seemed very rude, as if nobody had stopped to teach them manners.

After school, I would get dropped off from the bus near Granny's home with my two cousins, Iris and Jacob, who attended different schools in the same district as they were both older than me. Iris was a cherub-cheeked brunette with freckles covering her face, sprinkled under her plastic purple glasses. Jacob was a husky teenager with a blonde buzz cut that could've been a bully had he not been so kind. He may have been, but he was always nice to me. He thought it was his job to protect me.

Iris and Jacob would walk me to see Granny. Jacob spent most of his time in Papa's room practicing the trumpet, and Iris tried to make me play school with her, but I didn't like it. Sometimes Jacob would hang out with us and pick on Iris to make her stop trying to do the things that I didn't enjoy, like school or listen to her sing over the sound of the movie I was trying to watch. Jacob never annoyed me and tended to be quite comedic. He'd pick out new films I never thought to watch, like *Teenage Mutant Ninja Turtles* or other titles I had overlooked.

Iris wanted to watch unrealistic love stories that didn't seem to have a point, but I watched them with her anyway. Iris would smile tearfully and exclaim, "That'll be me one day!"

Watching her exuberate such enthusiasm and joy during the movies made it all worth it, even if I didn't see what she saw. She wanted to get married and have countless babies to love. She wanted to rescue the children who didn't have loving homes and felt she could do that when she became a famous singer.

We agreed on a few movies, like *'Titanic'* and *'Practical Magic,'* where my love story resided. *'Practical Magic'* felt different than any other love story, as if it were my own, my future. It's not the best love story, but in the end, she gets the guy of her dreams, the one that she thought didn't exist.

I had my first boyfriend in Kindergarten, a little boy named Ty, whose dad was friends with my dad and offered him a job working as a dump truck driver. Some days I would go to work with Dad on the weekends so I could hang out with Ty or be dropped off at Ty's house to spend the day with him and his family.

I watched fireworks with him for the first time on the back of his dad's truck. It ended when he told me one day on the school bus, "Hey, I have something to tell you."

I smiled, "What is it?"

He replied, "Well, there's this girl that comes over and cuts the grass. She's pretty and already grown up and everything, so I asked her to be my girlfriend. She said yes, so I'm going to have to break up with you because, well, she cuts my grass."

I never spoke to him until months later when an older boy was told to sit beside me on the bus. Iris was already sitting beside me at the window. Three people to a seat was severely overcrowded, especially since Iris was a bit heavy set and the boy was a teenager. Squished between the two of them on the tiny bus seat, I began to squirm and rock side to side, feeling suffocated by the two bodies sitting on my petite body. The boy put his hand on my thigh, but I swiped it away. After a moment, the boy decided to punch me hard on my thigh. I screamed in pain, causing the bus driver to stop. The boy changed seats since my cries were too loud to be next to him. He told the bus driver it was all my fault and I was the one that harmed him. Iris agreed since she had been busy staring out the window instead of what was happening.

As people got off at their stops, I sat by myself in the back of the bus, still crying from the pain. I didn't notice Ty sitting in front of me to the left until he turned around and he pulled a pretty teddy bear with a green dress out of his backpack. He handed it to me and said, "This is for you. I've been meaning to give it to you, but I hadn't found the right time. I'm sorry for what the mean boy did... also, I'm sorry for breaking up with you. I was stupid."

I whimpered as I hugged the bear and dried my tears in its fur.

Before getting off the bus, I weakly squeaked, "Thank you."

I hadn't noticed Ty since the day that he broke up with me. I thought he started getting rides to school from one of his parents, so he didn't have to face me. I never looked for him since it was obvious I meant nothing to him if he chose a teenage girl over me.

The bus driver called Dad, who showed up at Granny's house thirty minutes after I was dropped off from school, demanding details.

He said, "So I hear you got in a fight on the bus today with a high schooler, and you were the one that started it. Who was it? What happened?"

Sitting on the couch, I whimpered as I clutched the bear, "I didn't wanna fight. It was the mean boy."

He projected, "That's not what the bus driver said. He told me you started it, and it was with an older boy. You pinched him or something, so he hit you back?"

I insisted, "No, Daddy. The bus driver guy made him sit next to Iris and me, and it was really crowded, so I guess I might've been moving around too much. I just wanna breathe. He kept sitting too close to me. It's just too close. I didn't like it, but I didn't hurt nobody. He punched my leg!"

I showed him, "SEE?" I pulled up my pleated dress to show my thigh where the boy had left an already purpling bruise."

He huffed, "Okay, bet." He nodded at Iris to get her attention as he asked, "Hey, where's this boy live?"

She squeaked, "I think over on the next street."

Dad took me by my arm and moved me out the front door. We walked the streets of the trailer park as we searched for the boy, asking anyone, "Do you know the boy that hurt my girl?"

Most people didn't ride the bus, but occasionally he'd receive a finger point further down the second road of the trailer park until getting to Ty's house. Upon asking Ty, he pointed him across the street where the boy lived with his two parents. Dad got him to admit that he thought that I was annoying, so he decided to punch me. Bringing me with him to show his parents the victim of their son's brutality definitely reflected the severity of his punishment. The whipping from a belt could be heard halfway down the street, with the boy pleading for it to stop. It was a little harsh, but he lied and would get me in trouble when he had been cruel.

I thought nobody would believe me, let alone help me get justice.

Dad was my hero that day.

The bus driver was going to suspend me from the bus for a week, so Dad gave him a good talking-to as well. How a fifteen-year-old boy almost got away with hitting a five-year-old girl is a mystery, but Dad came to my defense. We spent most of that week together, and he almost didn't seem like a beast anymore.

A few months later, I was told we would move to a bigger house because I had a tiny brother growing in Mom's belly.

A week before the move, Jerry ran away to permanently be with this gray lady cat that kept strutting along the top of the fence line. He had run away with her before, but never for longer than a night at a time. He'd come back with deep scratches and broken bones as he was constantly getting in a merciless fight. The last time he came back after one of his late-night flings, he lost his left eye. With his eye unable to be saved, Mom poured peroxide in it to try to cleanse out the infection, but it only made Jerry give up his home and stay with his lady full time to be an alley cat. Mom helped me look for him the entire last week, putting up posters and knocking on all nearby doors to check if anyone had seen him. We had no luck, as nobody had noticed any cats roaming the streets.

Our new house was a massive brick home with a fenced-in backyard and trees to climb. It was a beautiful, lonely house on Robinwood Lane. My parents began their nightly quarreling once more, both defensive about how they spent their free time as they worked opposite hours at different jobs. Dad was a dump truck driver, and Mom was a late-night and sometimes early-morning waitress at *Waffle House*. Neither of them ever believed in one another to gain trust, and nothing had changed. Their arguments had just been more secretive, occurring when I hadn't been home, while I was in school, or with Granny. The peace I imagined filled with quiet nights was a hoax. There was nothing quiet that ever happened here.

3. Original Monster

On a night like any other, my parents were having another one of their screaming fights. I hadn't witnessed one personally for at least a year or two, but my ears always heard their quarrels in our new family home. Perhaps the size of the house made Dad think they couldn't be heard because of its size since the cacophony increased tremendously. Hiding from the sound in my closet made me feel like I was living in a deep, dark cave. The only imagery in my cave was through a flame emitting shadows with no proper form. What is the world in the light of a shadow? There is no sense of reality, no medium ground to create as a baseline to know what actually occurs. Each day, their bickering became more terrifying as I listened to the echoes fill the house with trepidation. Usually, I would never leave the safety of my room, but I grew frustrated trying to determine if danger was imminent or if it were all some kind of strange game that my parents played with one another. I decided to trespass on the battlefield.

Cautiously, I began my endeavor with slow and steady steps, looking throughout the hallway as if a landmine might detonate with one misstep. The walls around me were my barricade from open fire, yet even the walls themselves seemed treacherous. Ominous chaos vibrated the halls. A screeching howl burst through the kitchen, and I hurried my steps, tiptoeing while running simultaneously. The clamor was diagonal from me, just at the end of the hall. I took a shortcut through the kitchen, ducking to remain counter-level to avoid being seen. I slithered silently against the sanctuary of the shared wall between the kitchen and the dining room, peering from the corner of the destruction site.

Mom stood in the laundry room doorway, just before the stairs leading down to it. Dad stood in front of her, yelling brutishly at the top of his lungs. The sonority of their voices masked the words said to one another. Primitively, the one that makes the most noise is the one that possesses the most control.

I arrived just in time to hear Mom scream as the Beast laid his monstrous paws upon Mom's chest and pushed. Away she went, plummeting down the laundry room steps, collapsing onto the cement floor. Her gasp was caught between my lips, continuing the sound that would have come had she not fallen to the floor. It was like watching a horror movie in slow motion. I was the audience, incapable of any action to prevent the fall or move from the paralysis of shock. It was much worse than imagining the shadow puppets on the wall.

As the Beast turned his head towards me, the lens of my vision began to dizzily swirl through the halls. Forgetting the dangers that had eluded me before, I ran without the ability to run, as I stood seemingly frozen inside, yet cowardly running to the safety of my room. The only explosion that truly mattered had detonated upon my arrival. My fear of being seen trumped my concerns for Mom's health. The monster devours the witnesses because they have been caught watching their transformation, their most horrendous deeds. If the worst has already been seen, there is no use putting the darkness back into the shadows where it belongs. Once seen, all missiles deploy, and no one is immune.

I was destroyed, but my body was still intact, climbing up the sideways shelves of my closet until reaching the top. I nudged myself as close to the back wall as I could squeeze. I sat with my knees in my chest, my heart drumming through my skin. Once I caught my breath, I crouched, silent and invisible, listening for the sound of Mom's voice. All I could hear was a collateral of heedless crashing, the sound of bombs exploding until coming to an abrupt halt. Silence filled the doorways like the end had begun.

The pitter-patter of bare feet drew near, causing my heart

to beat dramatically. *Was I next?* Questions revolved within my mind. My father peered in the doorway of my room, looking for me in my bed. Had he seen me? I prayed, hopelessly, that he hadn't. With my heart beating sonorously, I prayed he could not hear it. My hands clutched at my chest to try to muffle the sound. To my reprieve, he forfeited his search before it truly began, only scanning through the door. His quickened pace echoed down the hall leading to his bedroom as he slammed his door shut. Moments later, I heard the door open with the quicked sound of 'tap-tap-tap' echoing out, racing to my room. A hand gripped the door frame, and its owner entered without hesitation. A form crept across the floor until reaching the closet.

A voice whispered, "Baby girl." Mom's worried voice repeated, "Baby girl come out."

I attempted my whistle, "Woo-hoo."

When she whistled back like a Mockingbird, I knew it was safe to come down. Before making my descent, I peeked my head from my safe place as I studied her face and movements to verify it was safe. She let out a relieved sigh, "There you are. Can you come down?"

I carefully made my way down the side beams to the ground where she stood. I stared at her as I worried, "Are you okay? Is it safe?"

Her gentle blue eyes pinned back impending tears. She looked up and sniffed the tears away so they wouldn't fall. She somberly replied, "I'm all right, baby. It was just a fight. It's all better now. Let me put you to bed."

I tucked myself into my blankets and climbed into bed while Mom picked up my *Minnie Mouse* music box from one of my shelves. She wound the music box as far as she could so it could play *'Once Upon A Dream'* to lull me to sleep. She took one last look at me before walking back to her room with the Beast.

Mom came to check on me after every one of their arguments. Mom and I knew something was different about this one, but the routine remained the same. Dad seemed to think that no one had feelings apart from himself, but Mom knew better. Every time they fought, I would hide, and she would find me.

Mom only put up with Dad's manipulations because it was the only part of his plan that seemed to work. Manipulation is just a game of delusion. In the end, nobody wins. He wanted to own her and Mom wanted to fly away. Her desire for freedom could not be contained.

The following day I was taken to my grandparent's house, as Mom needed to go to the hospital. Mom was having labor pains due to all of the chaos from the night before. A fall from the stairs by a pregnant woman is much more dangerous than simply getting harmed. Stress alone can cause a baby to be born prematurely. A fall has the potential to cause much more damage. Even death.

I spent the day watching movies and playing like I usually did while Granny sat in the kitchen staring at the phone on the kitchen desk. A little black notebook rested in her hands, compiled of names, numbers, and addresses. She stared at it blankly, unable to complete any action, uncertain whether there was good or bad news to spread. Instead, she chain-smoked cigarettes until it grew dark outside.

My birth almost killed my mom.

During my delivery, my heart rate dropped, and hers skyrocketed dangerously, so an emergency C-section had to take place to save us both. The doctors almost cut her stomach vertically in half instead of horizontally because of the urgency. Thankfully, a seasoned doctor stopped the surgery, realizing they would permanently damage her teenage body. Afterwards, the surgery was completed traditionally. Once I was removed from her body, we regained health. Her body was not meant to give birth since she had a retroverted uterus. Trying only led to possible complications.

I played alone all day without disturbing Granny. When it came to bedtime, I was a bit confused why Mom wasn't there to pick me up.

Granny told me that my baby brother was being born.

"Sometimes it takes a long time," she said.

I laid in bed next to Granny, staring at the box fan, and listening to its hum combined with the sleeping breath of Granny and the loud bear snores of my Papa, who slept on the other side of the bed. Granny's arm wrapped around me as I stayed up, pondering life's problems. How can a 5-year-old girl fix something as complicated as a monster?

This whole thing was Dad's fault. He pushed her down the stairs, and now Mom might be in danger at the hospital. Something needed to change. The monster needed to go. I spent the night pondering how until I drifted into a daze of slumber.

I spent the next day waiting for Papa to come in for the night. Once he finally did, he plopped himself down in his recliner and switched my movie to the evening news. Usually, I might complain, but I knew this is what he'd do. I waited for a commercial to begin and turned my head to look at him.

I softly but clearly asked, "Hey Papa… Papa, do you think you could fix a problem for me?"

His brow wrinkled, and his eyes turned towards me, confused and interrupted, but with a slight smile, he slurred, "You got me wrapped 'round and 'round your little finger. Anything for you."

I smiled, knowing that was exactly what he would say. I hesitated to ask the next part because it was wrong, but it was the only way.

I asked, "Papa, do you think you could kill my daddy for me?"

Tears filled his ocean eyes as the color of his face grew pale in shock. He held out his hand, motioning for me to come to him.

He choked, "Come here to me, baby girl. Talk to Papa. We'll talk and see."

I walked over to him hesitantly, worried I might be in trouble.

He coaxed, "It's okay, baby. Just come and sit. It's just a talk."

I sat beside him in his chair, with my legs in his lap. His arms wrapped around me for comfort, and we began to talk about why I felt compelled to ask him such a terrible thing.

He confessed, "I do anything for you, but there must be a good reason. If you just tell me if your dad hurt your mom, or if you touched you somewhere he's not supposed to. If he hurts you... I can only do this if he hurts you, my baby, baby girl."

I shook my head no and said, "I just want it done."

I could have given him an excuse and told him what I saw, but the most he could get me to say was he makes Mama sad.

He sighed and replied, "It's okay. You know, you're my favorite in the whole wide world. I just can't. Not for this."

I sat with him in his chair, continuing the news until Mama came to get me. When she came in, Papa took her back outside to talk. He told her what I had said and wanted to see if she would tell him anything I hadn't said to procure an excellent reason to be able to complete his task. There was nothing he wouldn't do for me. I never wanted Mom to know what I had asked. I just wanted it all to end.

Was it wrong? I never thought so, but perhaps the original monster was me. Or maybe I had just grown accustomed to the darkness. The only thing I knew without a doubt was it takes a monster to kill a monster.

4. Feeding On Fear

Paralyzed with fear, I spied the gray-fleshed hunchback pacing across the threshold of my bedroom door. Once the house grew silent, the anticipation of its arrival kept me awake until it faded into the doorframe, slowly like a shadow, until it showed its proper form.

Folds of skin hung off its ribs and sagged into a pot belly cradled with skinny snake-like arms. It was naked, yet sexless. I never saw it smile as it hid its perilous grin with its cupped, taloned claws. I named my creature the 'Laughing Monster' for the way it hissed as it paced, snickering so hard that it vibrated reverently as it walked.

All I could do was stare and wish for my fuzzy hero to banish it from wherever it came from. If he could save me, he would.

The only peaceful nights I had were when Tommy was allowed to sleep with me. He'd cradle my legs and purr me to sleep. On the nights I couldn't sleep, Tommy would follow me into the living room and sit beside me. We'd watch television consisting of old horror movies, or recurring reruns of I Love Lucy or M.A.S.H. He'd follow me back into my room when I was finished and resume his position at my feet. Tommy seemed aware that I needed protection, but he couldn't help that he was only allowed when my parents let him out of their room. Other times he was away from home, prowling the streets for food allotted in garbage bins since cat food isn't very savory.

Tommy came home after a long night of rummaging through the neighborhood garbage and was poisoned by a neighbor's trash. He only returned home to say goodbye as he died in Mom's arms.

I didn't see him pass away or watch him be buried in the backyard. I was told what happened later that day when I asked where Tommy was.

Going to bed that night was nothing short of a heart-wrenching nightmare. The yowling cries of Tommy's corpse circling the house was all that I could hear. It was like a wolf screaming at the moon in our yard. At times it felt like he was still alive and desperately wanted in. His paw tapped at my window, pleading for an invitation. How could I deny my protector? All he wanted was to be with me, to say goodbye one last time... but I knew it wasn't really him. Tommy had died, and an impostor was using his body to try to break in... But why? Without a soul inhabiting his body, I couldn't let the darkness win.

After that night, I wasn't as afraid of my laughing monster. I had denied the dybbuk possessing the bones of my loving protector, and it couldn't get much more terrifying than that. My laughing monster no longer had control over my fear. It was just something I didn't enjoy, a bad experience on repeat.

Boredom creates complacency, so my monster invited some friends to spice things up. It paced while shadows all around me crowded my room. Sometimes they gathered so closely that it was difficult not to touch one, even while lying in bed. Touching a shade of darkness is like feeling a frozen area of the room. It turned my skin to goosebumps and stole the oxygen for my lungs, but that was all. Just a sudden discomfort accompanied by the thought, *Don't do that again.* I felt claustrophobic in my shadow-infested room, but it was insignificant compared to hearing Tommy's cries for help.

Something compelled me to look under my bed. A large black form with spiny legs was discovered, stumbling clumsily without enough room to crawl. Its diamond eyes glowed white as it looked at me and gruffed, "It's me, Batman."

I screamed, unable to hold back another emotion.

Mom rushed in, panting, "What's wrong? What's wrong, baby? Are you okay? What happened?"

It had all gotten too real to tolerate. I had seen Batman in television commercials, but I had never visualized anything unoriginal. Batman wasn't supposed to be a tangible form. If any cartoon had to live under my bed, why him? I didn't even want to watch him on television.

I squealed, "Batman. It's Batman underneath my bed!

She tried desperately not to laugh before she cooed, "Sweetheart, you don't need to be afraid of Batman. He's a good guy. He fights crime."

I erupted, "I don't care if he's good, bad. I don't care. He needs to get out from under the bed. He scared me. It's bad enough with everyone else in here. But him? ...I'm trying to go to bed, and they never, ever leave me alone. He can't be good. He's a bad, bad Batman."

I was exhausted by all the chaos surrounding bedtime. Mom pursed her lips together and smiled through them as she tilted her head, trying to understand all the words I had just said without laughing. She whispered, "Hold on, baby girl." She left my room and returned shortly after with a bottle of perfume labeled *'Poison.'*

She sprayed a few pumps of perfume underneath my bed and all around the room and beamed, "Ta-da. Now all the monsters are gone, even Batman! This bottle here is monster spray. It's magic. When you feel scared or see a monster, spray them with this, and they'll be gone. Poof! It's yours. It'll keep you safe."

She smiled as she turned my bedroom light off and shut my door to a soft close, leaving it cracked open just an inch to let some light in. In the next room, I could hear an explosion of laughter, but I tried to ignore it and get some rest. Mom was making fun of me and telling all of her friends. Apparently, my parents were having a party, and my fear was the new joke.

The following nights were easier. Believing I had some power helped me feel like I had the upper hand on the monsters. Even with a sense of relief, I wasted a third of the bottle within a week. The darkness prefers to be kept from being sanitized as it's disheveled, coming from a world of tar and sickness. So it worked well in the shadows because it was an alcohol-based perfume. Still, my laughing monster only faded partially on the areas where the spray spritzed but never missed a step, regardless of how often I saturated it with Poison. It didn't keep me from trying to make it disappear. Hence why all the perfume disappeared so quickly. Once the perfume bottle was empty, Mom replaced it with a spray bottle filled with water with a taped-on label that read, 'Monster Spray'. The idea was supposed to relax my mind and be effective as a placebo, but it didn't fool the monsters so it didn't work for me. I wanted more of the real poison.

Explaining how it didn't work did nothing but lead to the lie, "It works the same. It's just in a bigger bottle."

It's impossible to explain that monsters are real. No one believes you.

I forgot that I attended school by the time first grade began. I was going to a new school a few blocks away from home. Mom showed me the way to school with a ride in her car.

When returning home, Mom informed me, "So that's how you get to school. You'll be walking, so it's important to always follow the same path so you won't get lost. Do you think you'll remember?"

I sat speechless in the car and looked all around me as if somehow I could see the path if I had just looked around enough times. I held my hands out dramatically on each side of myself and shrugged, showing I had no idea where to go.

Mom giggled and assured me, "Don't worry baby girl. I'll walk with you on your first day."

Mom walked with me to school the first week and occasionally walked me home the second to ensure my arrival and departure. After that, I was on my own.

She reminded me, "Remember, never talk to strangers,

even if they talk to you first. And nev-er, ev-er get in the car with one, never. I don't care what they tell you, even if they tell you they have a sweet little kitten you can pet if you just get in, offer you candy, or even say that they know me. Even if they say something bad happened to me, or I said it was okay for you to go. Remember, never get in a car with strangers. Oh, and always take the same path home," she smiled, "Capiche?"

I nodded in agreement, "Yes, Mama. I understand."

My walks to school were usually peaceful. Strangers rarely tried to talk to me, nor were they around. A car never stopped to pick me up. My only issue was the stray dogs rummaging around the neighborhood. Sometimes they chased me halfway to school and on the way back home. I was terrified. I prayed a stranger would come and help me so I wouldn't have to run or be afraid, never knowing when the dogs would appear.

One time a rottweiler chased me home. I came in panting and slammed the door. Dad was standing in the living room.

He asked, "What are you doing? Why are you breathing so hard?"

I stammered, "It's a dog, a really big dog. It chased me home. It was going to eat me! It won't go away."

His brow wrinkled, and he opened the front door to check. As he closed the door, he chuckled, "Bullshit. That dog? That dog scared you so much you had to run home? Get real. You're not a baby anymore."

I frowned in confusion, ashamed, as I walked to the door to see what he meant. A Chihuahua stood at the end of the sidewalk, barking incessantly. Dad closed the door and raised an eyebrow, his green eyes glowing in rage. He thought I was lying, making up stories about things I saw, as he believed I did as a pastime with all the walking nightmares.

He barked again, "Bullshit. What, you thought I wouldn't check? You lie worse than your mom."

I let out a frustrated grunt as I opened the door again, determined to prove him wrong. When I opened the door, the massive black dog that chased me stood next to the Chihuahua, taking turns barking.

Dad sighed, "Just closed the door. You know, next time, just stand still. Dogs can only see in black and white, so you blend in with your surroundings when you stand still. They only see the objects in motion. Like a ball. They never play with a ball that sits still."

I'm not sure where he got his information from, but it certainly wasn't from a dog.

Standing still only creates an easier target. Luckily, two strangers helped me on a morning stroll the next time I encountered a dog. Before I could try out Dad's advice, they shooed it away as I attempted to stand still. I stopped having dog problems. After that, I often saw them on my walk to school, moving their walking route to mornings to help keep an eye on me. Strangers weren't quite as bad as Mom had claimed. Maybe she had just met the wrong kind of strangers. If I passed by them, we said hello.

First grade was a difficult time. The coursework was simple, but socializing with the other kids was impossible. Recess was a travesty. I couldn't play on the playset because a strange-looking girl took tyranny over it. If anyone stepped foot on it, she would pull their hair so hard it hurt their neck. Why was I the only one that took her hair in hand and pulled it in return? No teacher ever stopped to help when it was done to me, so why did three teachers rush over when her black wig fell to the ground?

One snipped, "Don't do that! How could you?"

I whined, "But she pulled my hair first."

The teacher shook her head, scowling, "That doesn't matter if she hurt you first. You go tell someone! You do not pull her hair in return. What good does that do? She can't even feel it. She has to wear her hair like a hat. She's different, not like you. She's special. You need to sit by us in time out for the rest of recess."

Special didn't compute to me. I wasn't aware that anyone had different levels of functioning from anybody else. I only wanted to go down the slide on the jungle gym, but nobody could since the girl ruled over the area. She never even went down the slide. She just kept watch in the middle, pacing as she waited to pull the next person's hair when they tried to intrude on her playing field. It was terribly unfair.

I learned my lesson and stopped trying to use the jungle gym. I took my attention to the swings. All of the swings were empty, so it seemed like the perfect place to play.

Unfortunately, you had to pass by a large shade tree to get to the swings. Under the shade tree stood a group of boys. I muttered, "Excuse me."

The boys just stood under the tree and stared at me as I was unable to pass through without them moving. I tried to walk around them until one of the boys jumped in front of me. He jested, "You look like a horse. Don't she?" He looked around at the other boys, who nodded in agreement.
He grinned, "Yeah! You know what they do to horses, don't cha?" He jumped on my back, wrapping his arms around my neck, and his legs straddled my unformed hips. I spun in a circle, trying to throw him off my body.

I screeched, "Get off. Stop it! I'm not a horse! Get off me!"

Once a boy was thrown off, another took his place, yelling, "Giddy up horsey!"

The cycle continued for two weeks straight. I was hoping they'd get tired of bullying me. It was the same thing every day. No one ever stopped them. Maybe the teachers thought it was some sort of twisted game. But it definitely couldn't have seemed like I was having any fun at all.

There was nothing left to do at recess. It was nothing like the park.

I decided to walk during recess instead of trying to play. I couldn't do anything anyway. I wasn't allowed to. What did the other kids do anyway? Most of them went on walks as well. It was all that could be done if you weren't a bully. Only one kid went down the slide after getting their hair pulled and didn't go back for another round. The swings remained empty aside from the boys under the tree that bullied anyone that tried to pass.

I tried to make friends with a group of girls, but when I asked if they wanted to play, a blonde girl in the middle snorted, "My Mommy said we're not allowed to talk to strangers. If you're not one of us, then you're a stranger. We've all been friends since we were babies. I don't know you."

I'm not sure what was wrong with the kids at this school. Everyone walked separately, moving like zombies in a field. The programming begins early.

The final night I saw my monster, I woke up from a dead sleep with an incessant itch on my face. My nose felt like it had become an ant mound.

I wiggled my arm free from under the blankets that swaddled me so I could scratch my nose. I clawed at the base of my nose, where the itch seemed the most intense.

Crawling prickled over my entire face like an eruption of tiny spines. If anything about the sensation felt remotely pleasant, I would say it even tickled.

That being said, without the pleasantries, it was a disgusting tickling swarming my entire face. I felt a new itch upon the hand that I had scratched my nose with. It crawled up my arm until I shook it off. I watched the black insect scurry into hiding across my sheets. My skin was on fire. Was there a fire? Does fire itch?

I sniffed the air to check for the odor of smoke and began to asphyxiate. My hands pulled at the moist flesh inside my mouth, trying to clear my airways as I retched. I gagged until small crunchy particles began to fall from my mouth, covered in spit. The choking decreased the more I choked up until I forced more coughs to entirely expunge whatever had caused my breathing to constrict.

I felt like I was drowning. My throat burned up to my nasal cavity. My fingers crawled at the carcasses crushed within my mouth, pulling them out with my hands as far as I could reach, one splintered leg at a time. What sort of darkness had buried itself in my face?

The bitter taste of blood and burnt licorice overpowered my senses. I couldn't get the taste out of my mouth. The moldy odor of stale dirt filled my nostrils. I tried to push the foul stench out, blowing my nose in my hands to flush them out. A body crawled down upon my lips until hot tears fell from my eyes and burned down my cheeks. The bug crawled out from my hair. Was it ever going to end?

The taction of my own tears sickened me. I felt the inside of my mouth again in an attempt to purify their pieces from my tongue and teeth and all other surrounding tissue in between. I pulled an egg case out from underneath my tongue as I stifled my vomit from violent expungement. I felt inside my nose with both pinkies to check the passages were clear. My hands collapsed around my throat as I spotted what creature had infested my face. *There was no good answer.*

Roaches. Disgusting, ugly, dirty cockroaches had made a nest inside of my face. How was that even possible? Taking a breath, I dusted my arms, shook my hair out, and felt at my body until I was satisfied there were no more bugs. I felt relief momentarily until I remembered I had ear holes.

Please, no more. I don't know where they all came from, but please let them all be gone.

I pulled one last whole cockroach from my left ear. It squirmed, running with its legs between my index finger and thumb. I threw it to the ground and covered my face as I sobbed.

Why had I just let that bastard live?!

I stood up and rushed over to the light switch to examine the crime scene on my bed. Crushed pieces of roaches lay in a swarm on my sheets. No live insects were found. I desperately scrubbed at the insect grave composed of tiny ligaments in my bed. I couldn't just lay on top of them. They had to be removed. It was too disturbing. I picked every last fragment from my sheets with my bare fingers, scrubbing the residue from my sheets with my nails.

I turned off the light and covered my body with my head buried inside my blanket, my pillow on top of my face, swaddling myself like an airtight container. It felt like wax was covering my teeth, a coating of bodies that would never come clean. I tried to scrub my teeth with my tongue, but it didn't help. I only absorbed more of the waxy stench of burning dirt-covered, moldy licorice. I could not escape the thought that I had just been dubbed a perfect roach den.

How could my body betray me?

As I looked over to my door, I heard the laughing monster snicker one last time. His body had become shadow-like smoke within the door. I never saw the laughing monster again. This was his final farewell, as he had finally won.

In the morning, I felt the crawling haunt me, so I confessed to Mom what had occurred last night.

Mom dismissively hushed, "That's gross. I'm sorry, babe. That sounds like a terrible dream."

I pleaded, "No, Mama, it really happened,"

She repeated, "It was just a bad dream. It didn't happen. That is that. Umm... I hope you have a wonderful day at school and can forget all about it."

Memories of my parents not believing me have mostly been expunged from my mind. I recollect only clips of my father bellowing, "Bullshit," but for why it all fades.

All I know is if I was in trouble, "Bullshit!" If I saw something he didn't believe, it was all such "Bullshit!" It was his catchphrase, and I made him say it at least two times a day, if not twenty.

Mom tried to understand, but it was challenging to maintain a calm demeanor when nothing seemed to make it go away. My delusions never stopped, and it was beginning to be too much to handle.

Mom took me to spend some time with my grandparents a couple days after my face had been infested. Unbeknownst to me, my parents were bombing our house for the roaches infesting our house.

Had I been told, I may not have felt so terribly misunderstood.

All I could think was, *nobody believes you. You're a dirty liar. Bullshit! Why did you make it up?*

Why did I even wake up? Had I just stayed asleep, maybe somebody could see what had happened to me. Unless, of course, it didn't happen. Then why did I make it up? Because I didn't. I couldn't. I felt it.

I don't know what's real anymore.

I tried to watch a cartoon to forget about it but wasn't interested in anything. I wanted to tell myself it didn't matter. Not the event, disbelief, my mind, or anything else. If nothing at all matters, then why exist at all?

Sitting on the living room floor, the sweetest voice I had ever heard purred, *All is not lost, little one. Breathe in slowly. Breathe in the light of my star, and know everything matters. Everything you see and feel is there for a reason. I know it's hard. It feels impossible sometimes. Just know that you matter. Have you told everyone? If you tried, someone here might believe you. Breathe and just try. If all else fails, know that I believe you.*

I smiled, feeling the soothing light brighten the room. It only began to fade on the last word. I had heard this voice before, staring out into the night sky. Was this the voice of God or the voice of my star?

I stood up slowly and crept into the kitchen, where Granny sat with her face in her hands, trapped in her world of thoughts. Maybe she could help me get out of my thoughts since she spent so much time in hers.

I stammered, "Granny..."

She sighed, "Go play, baby doll."

I tried again, taking a small step back until I gained confidence, and walked over to her instead of backing away.

I gently rubbed her back and whispered, "I know you have a lot on your mind, but I have a lot on mine too. I just like to talk about something. Maybe you could help me. It won't take too long. I don't want to bother you if it's too much."

She pulled her head from her hands to sit up and smiled gently, "No, it's okay. You're no bother. What did you want to talk about? I'll listen."

I took a deep breath and began, "So I have this problem. It's okay if you don't believe me. I don't…well, I just… Do you think it's possible, just even possible, that when you're sleeping, a bug or lots of bugs could get in your mouth when you sleep?"

I cringed, waiting for a response while Granny looked to the side to think until she looked at me and nodded, "Sure. I don't see why not. Why? Did that happen to you?"

My eyes filled with tears as I nodded my head yes and cleared my throat. I looked up to put my tears back behind my eyes like the grown-ups did to try not to cry.

Granny put her arm around me and hushed, "It's okay, baby doll. Why don't you tell me about it? Maybe it'll make you feel better."

I told her what happened in great detail, ending with, "…I told Mama, but she said it was just a bad dream. It was much more real than that. Please, just don't tell Mama. She doesn't believe it. I don't want her to feel mad. I just can't forget about it. It was horrible."

She smiled, "It's okay, sweet girl. I'll keep it between us girls."

I smiled and skipped into the living room, relieved that somebody finally believed me. I didn't feel so alone anymore. Mom came to get me just a couple hours afterwards. She walked into the kitchen to talk to Granny.

I wasn't alarmed until I heard Mom shout, "…But she made it up! It didn't happen! I can't believe she told you that. It didn't even happen!"

I had never heard Mom shout at Granny before. It was all my fault.

It was a silent drive home as I admired how at least one person I loved believed me. Even if, at that moment, the person I love most was growing resentful of me.

When we arrived home, roaches covered the walls since the roach bomb had finished smoking. The stumbling bugs covered the walls of every room in the house.

Was my story believable now?

Nothing was said, just hushed complaints between my parents about how to further get rid of all the bugs as I was told to go to my room.

The next couple of weeks were spent in my room due to a stomach ailment. I presumed it was due to the infestation that had occurred in my face. I couldn't eat or stay out of the bathroom for any extent of time. Water went right through me. Mom constantly tried to feed me chicken noodle soup, even as I sat on the toilet. The constant expungement was excruciating. I secreted so much into the latrine that my excrement turned white, containing no waste, only stomach bile.

I was rarely taken to the doctor, but this sickness required an emergency room visit. I was prescribed suppositories that felt even more repulsive than the sickness itself. Feeling it melt inside my rectum was almost as bad as a face full of roaches.

Who invents rectal medication? What kind of doctor prescribes this to a six-year-old? I would have preferred to stay in the bathroom. At least while the drug worked, I could be sick in my room and play video games as much as I liked.

5. Home Sweet Dungeon

Life began to change suddenly after I met the first person I disliked upon sight.

What dark shadow of a fat man sat on the couch in our living room? Why did he look like some sort of giant bug? I tried to imagine what kind of bug.

A dung beetle? A spider? Maybe a cockroach. I couldn't decide.

His oversized glasses were the same color as an American cockroach, brown with gold tint, aviation style. His shirt was the same color, neatly tucked into his black pants, held up by a leather belt. His stomach protruded like an umbrella over his pants.

It could be called a 'Santa belly' had there been anything 'jolly' about him.

When he smiled, it seemed sideways, like the other side of his face couldn't quite match up to smiling because it was a farce. His eyes were void of any trace of light, like an eerie dark night without a single star with a moon that would never rise.

His soulless eyes peered at me with a crooked smile. He stood up and walked over to where I stood in the doorway beside Mom.

He spoke nasally, "Hello, little girl. Would you like to come live with me?"

I snapped, "No, I don't think so!"

I tried to run away, but Mom blocked the door with her arm.

She sternly retorted, "No, Annie. That was very rude. Would you like to try that again?"

I barked, "I meant what I said, and I said what I meant. I'm not rude. You're rude. He's rude. I'm going to my room. Don't try and stop me."

She removed her arm and huffed, "Well, fine. Go to your room then... And don't tell Daddy."

When I reached the outside of my bedroom door, I turned around and smiled cruelly, "Why not tell Daddy?"

I vanished into my room as she gasped in surprise.

How dare she ask me to be polite to a shadow? Wasn't I supposed to not talk to strangers? There was nothing stranger than him! Not for his appearance but for the general air that surrounded him. For the dirty aura leaving him colorless, only holding the odor of an electrical fire.

Mom was leaving Dad, and we would live with this strange, abhorrent man.

Why had Mom chosen some distorted villain instead of the prince I had envisioned for her? She could have easily chosen better, but the choice had already been made.

When the news became official, Dad wanted to meet the man, Rob, whom Mom was going to leave him for.

Dad made a big barbeque that we all enjoyed outside by the pool. Dinner went over so well that we went swimming in our pool afterwards. I thought we were all having fun, playing games like Marco-Polo and seeing how long each of us could hold our breath. Upon Rob's turn to hold his breath, I decided to see if I could assist. I stood on Rob's back as if he were a surfboard.

Rob tried to come up for air, but I kept my balance, only adding variance to my surfing game. It was like going over a big wave.

Finally, he exploded from the water, his black eyes bugging out of his head as he raged, "You tried to kill me! Are you fucking crazy?! Bride of Chucky, mother fucker. Why did you do that?"

He looked around at the surprise on both of my parents' faces until Dad began to grin.

Rob spat, "She tried to kill me. Did neither of you see that? Why didn't you stop her? I could've drowned."

Mom grabbed me by my arm and dragged me out of the pool. Dad was growling at Rob when we got to the patio door. I'm not sure what was said, just that I had disappointed in my mom again. At least Dad was proud of me.

When we got to my room, she scolded, "What on earth were you trying to do out there?"

I shrugged, "I thought we were playing a game."

She shook her head in disappointment and left me in my room. She went back outside to manage the erupting chaos.

I was the nasty little demon child trying to drown a grown man. How terrifying it must have been to be inundated by 40 pounds in four feet of water. Rob only survived because he fortuitously stood up.

My father was never as scary as I perceived him to be. He was overly boisterous, held Mom hostage, and took his entire life with his family for granted... But that night, he was only a sorrowful, lonely man who was losing his family. He could not keep the endless stream from falling from his eyes.

I spent the last night alone with Dad in his room. Everything had already been moved out, apart from his things. I felt relieved to spend the night with him because it was the day after the pool party fiasco. I was dreading moving in with this Rob. I had only carved a path of destruction if I were to live with him. The television played the movie *Young Guns 2* on repeat.

Dad sobbed, "Annie, baby girl, are you going to miss me when you're gone?"

I took a breath and thought about how I wanted to answer.

Should I be honest and reply no? I have been praying for ages for mom to leave you. I even asked Papa to kill you. She chose the wrong person to replace you because he seems even worse than you, but I'm not sure I'll miss you.

Honesty is not what anyone wants from me.

Instead, I replied, "Of course, Daddy, I love you."

My reply must not have seemed exceptionally convincing, so he mumbled. "What are you... What will you miss about me?"

I pondered until he whimpered, "Tell me a good memory. Tell me about all the good times we had together."

I hummed a sigh, "We had lots of good times. I have lots of good memories."

He stopped crying to listen, his eyes glowing bright with a hint of impatience.

I hurried, "I remember when you'd make dinner and tell me I ate *Bugs Bunny* and *Bambi*. And one time, you told me we were eating giraffe neck. I told my teacher at school she should try it because it's good. She called you because she was worried we were eating giraffes. You told me it was really beef tenderloin and to make sure to tell my teacher the next morning. I make you laugh sometimes."

He chuckled, "It never bothered you. You're so tough. No matter what I told you, you'd say it was delicious.

I continued as he smiled cheerfully, "Sometimes you lift me up really high and fly me around the house. I could even touch the top of the door. One time we went to Six Flags, and you told me we were going to see Uncle Fud, but I didn't have an Uncle Fud. It was a good surprise. You're so funny. We rode a really big roller coaster, but it was scary.

He huffed, "It wasn't scary. You liked it. You're my brave girl."

I shrugged. I ran out of memories, even though he urged me for more. I fell asleep on his chest, covered by a river of his tears.

Had he been the person he was that night, I bet I could have loved him.

My new life consisted of being closed in a room alone in Rob's new house. I couldn't say what the house looked like on the outside or whether it was a house, trailer, or broom closet with a trap door.

At first, my door wasn't locked. It just had a strange taupe-colored plastic speaker box attached to the top corner of the door, which caused a deafening security alarm to trigger when the door opened and wouldn't cease until the key was placed in its lock. Sometimes that took moments. Other times, hours. It depended on what they were doing, if the key could be found and if they were even home.

The siren on my door was my tyrannical babysitter. It didn't always keep me from getting out despite the sound, so a lock was installed outside the door. The two child keepers (the outer lock and alarm box) ensured I couldn't do anything or leave my room unless a grown-up came in and asked if I wanted a shower, bathroom break, or food. It definitely cut down on the price of keeping me alive.

I wondered if somehow I died right now... how long would it take until somebody noticed? Would anyone even be sad if I stopped living? Would there even be a funeral, or would I be thrown away with the garbage and forgotten?

My baby brother, Orion, started spending time in the room with me once he began to walk. I had never spent any time with him. I rarely had the opportunity to look at or touch him, so feeding, changing his diapers, and keeping him happy was overwhelming. Especially since I couldn't leave the room.

Every other day Orion was put in my room to be watched by the security system and me. They needed some alone time and had three excellent ways of forgetting he existed. My room was the place where children disappeared and were forgotten until it was convenient.

How nice that must be to not have enough time alone.

The better Orion walked and babbled, the more time he spent caged up with me until the room was no longer mine but ours.

I was given a slew of diapers, wipes, and a container of baby food so he wouldn't have any problems. Sometimes I was tempted to eat the baby food, but I never went through with it.

It was barely enough to feed Orion, depending on how long he stayed with me in the abyss.

Some days he was with me for so long that he ran out of diapers and cried for more food. I showed him how sometimes you have to pee on the floor. I didn't have a solution for food, but he began to catch and eat cockroaches that were sometimes found crawling through the door.

How could I stop him when we had no food?

I tried to save one last diaper for bedtime, so there wouldn't be any accidents. If he had extra diapers, we'd both use a diaper for a toilet because we had no way of emptying our bladders any other way. The door was constantly locked, and if not, the alarm would blare ruthlessly.

The dark shadow of a man controlled our every move. I rarely ever saw Mom.

My situation never changed, regardless of my Mom's location or my behavior. Orion received more freedom since he was only a year old. Every moment Mom had time for a child, she gave it to Orion. I can't be sure if it was because he was a baby or if she just liked him more.

I was a prisoner, a grown-up, without needing a hug or someone to even notice me. I didn't need the human touch. I was like an old, drooling dog that should be put down. My only use was to feed and change Orion. I received no thanks or reward for it. I did it out of the goodness of my heart. Nobody deserves to be treated like I was. I did everything I could to not let him know he was caged. My room became a prison of filth that disgusted the people who gave me food. Without appropriately timed bathroom breaks, there was nothing left to do but continually pee on the carpet. Sometimes I'd be given the opportunity when, moments before, I had already gone. If I declined to go, my bathroom privileges would be revoked for the night.

I no longer had parents, just people that came to the door.

One day I came up with the most brilliant plan. If my brother and I piled toys into the air vent on our bedroom floor, the toys could help us escape, like in *Toy Story*. I knew it was unrealistic, but they might if I prayed really hard.

Compliance was getting me nowhere. The idea was to pile toys into the vent until the weight of the toys collapsed the hose inside. We never had to be caged up again if there was a giant hole in the floor.

I never thought how we would fit through the little vent hole. I didn't think that part through.

A toy never came to the rescue, and the vent never collapsed. The mass of toys, however, clogged up the vent until we didn't have any toys left, and no cold air came through. The room became a stench-filled sauna from the humidity and the piss-covered carpet. Nothing was clean. It went unnoticed for weeks until I woke up to Mom shouting as I laid cuddled on my blanket bed on the floor with Orion, covered in one another's feces. Nobody had been home, so I wasn't allowed bathroom access that night or given more baby supplies.

When Mom returned home, she decided to check on us.

You can only hold your bowels for so long before they simply explode. It was a revolting mess, an absolute shit show.

We were shaken awake and bathed together as Mom whined, "Whyyy? Ugh! So gross. Ew! Ew! Ew! Next time use the toilet, capiche? If you changed your brother's diapers more often, this wouldn't happen."

How? What could anyone else expect? Next time I'll just walk right out the bolted screeching door and use the toilet. Sure, I'll use the diapers that Orion ran out of hours ago. I was asleep, so you never know when a diaper will explode, even if he still had any. How was I supposed to potty-train a two-year-old without a bathroom?! Was that my job? I held back a slew of raging thoughts as my brain began to boil.

Mom's fingers scrubbed the fecal matter from my hair as I replied, "Okay."

She smiled and tugged at my hair as she repeated, "Capiche?"

I dryly replied, "Sure, I'll try."

She sighed dramatically and scrubbed my body more

aggressively until she determined we were clean. I was given a single sheet to make into a bed because all the blankets were dirty now. Orion was taken back to Mom's room since I did a terrible job caring for him.

I could not help but be resentful of my infant brother. I missed Mom less with every short moment spent with her. I still loved her for the angel she was, but not the ghost she was becoming.

I was just tired of being held hostage without an end. I was exhausted from being the only one acting as a mother to a baby when I was a baby myself. I got nothing for it aside from a black hole expanding in my stomach with every day that passed, and was kept prisoner. I only received fewer blankets and more time alone in the abyss of my horrendous room.

My entrapment was about to end. We were moving, and my eighth birthday was coming soon. Mom and Rob needed a week to prepare, so I spent a week with my aunt Claire and cousin Iris. Driving up to my aunt's trailer, my mom saw a friend, so she got out to walk while the car continued to drive the rest of the way to my aunt's house. My mom hugged her friend for an extended time and cheerfully walked with him to meet us at Claire's trailer. Her friend was a slender old man with long gray hair and wrinkled skin. She said goodbye to him and walked inside Claire's trailer. Mom briefly asked my aunt to keep an eye on me, saying I wouldn't need anything extra and drove off with her master and Orion without as much as a goodbye.

6. Vacation and Worms

For a week, I shared Iris's room with her. Iris had short brown hair, hazel eyes, and large visible freckles speckled across her cheeks, outlining her glasses. The two of us happily cuddled in bed together each night. I hadn't slept in a real bed in a year or more.

Time doesn't exist when you're caged inside with no expectation of freedom. A day can feel as long as a month. It felt like I had been shoved inside my repugnant room for at least four years. I wasn't even sure how old I was. I had all but forgotten my star in the night sky.

Iris and I walked to a nearby lake every day to swim and explore the shoreline. We even discovered an abandoned canoe on the shore during one of our expeditions. Ten feet from the shore, I had a sneaking suspicion there was a hole in the boat, even though there wasn't any water leaking in. The further we floated from shore, the deeper the canoe seemed to sink into the water. I had a newly developed fear of gars. I only knew about them because Iris told me gars are legless alligators that live in lakes, in *this* lake in particular, before we got in the boat and rowed off from shore. I thought I could be brave, but with each passing moment, I couldn't help but think about gars tipping the boat or the boat sinking, leaving us in the deepest part of the lake.

How could I not be afraid? I didn't want to die by slowly being eaten alive or drowned while a gar trusted me in the water with an alligator roll.

My cousin squealed when I jumped out, and the boat rocked, but she jumped out after me a few moments later. She never left me behind, even if I was just being paranoid.

53

Iris was always telling me scary stories during our trips to the lake. There was a metal building sitting on a part of the lake shore, so I asked, "What do you think is in there?"

Iris inquired, "Over where?"

I explained as I pointed at the metal shed, "In there. The light isn't normally on, but it is today. What do you think is in there?"

Iris smiled, "That… is the boat house. This is Possum Kingdom Lake. It's where the dark secrets are kept. Murders and whatnot. It's best not to look if you don't want to be the next victim."

"Oh," is all I could think to reply until I grew curious again and asked, "How do you know?"

Iris laughed under her breath and replied, "I saw someone die, and they were taken there, to that shed."

I gasped, "They didn't see you?"

She smiled, "They did, but I told him I didn't want to die and I'd never tell his secret. I never have until I told you, so now you know. It's best just to stay away from there."

Iris introduced me to her boyfriend, Corey, and his younger brother Chris. She brought us all into her room to show me how grown-ups make out with a game called thirty minutes in heaven. She put Chris and I in her closet with the idea we might mimic them. Chris and I just sat in the closet, holding hands with one another, with our backs towards them, facing the wall instead of watching them ravish one another.

After a few minutes, Chris asked, "Are we supposed to do that?"

I looked over my shoulder to peer through the shutters of the closet door to see what was happening in the bedroom. Iris sat on top of Corey with her shirt off, moving her hips back and forth against his body. She was dramatically groaning as their lips slobbered all over one another.

I raised an eyebrow and pursed my lips together as I

whispered, looking back at the wall, "I don't think I'd like that."

He smiled and rubbed his thumb across my hand. Iris wanted us to do all the same things together, but I spent enough time being expected to act like I was a grown-up. I just wanted to be a seven-year-old girl with the freedom to explore the world around me. Maybe she was just allowing me to explore something else with nothing being pushed on us too severely. It was just an option with video guidance if we wished to follow along.

When Iris and Corey were finished, the closet door was pulled open suddenly.

Iris shouted, "Gotcha!"

Chris and I looked behind us, surprised by the sudden burst of light.

What did she think she would find?

We were just two kids in a closet holding hands and occasionally whispering to one another.

I fell in love with Chris the first day I met him. He was kind, gentle, and never asked me to do anything I didn't want to do. Sometimes we'd kiss, but never as aggressively as Iris did with Corey. Chris was quiet, shy, and often fell victim to bullying, which made us very similar.

His parents were abusive, spending too much time giving him violent punishment and telling him to stay in his room or else. He often escaped his house through the doggy door. I was proud of him for finding a way to escape, even as I wished there had been a doggy door when I was trapped. We should have run away together to escape our parental imprisonment, even though we were both too little to truly know how to survive. As long as we had each other, I bet we would have been alright. Oysters were abundant in the lake, and if we were prepared, I bet we could kill a gar and feast on it for at least two days. It would have been a life of adventure, but neither of us asked the other if they would, afraid the answer might be no. It was risky, but life at home was already dangerous for him and miserable for me. What could be the harm of living as wildlings?

I woke up every day next to Iris, missing Chris's smile, gentle brown eyes, and soft-spoken voice. How could anyone hurt such an innocent, handsome boy?

Every day was an adventure wherever we wanted to explore. Chris would go everywhere with Iris and me whenever he found a way to escape or was allowed to be free from his room. We went to the lake, walked around the trailer park, and once snuck into a random yard to grab a peach. I received my first bee sting that way. I thought a thorn had gotten me, leaving a big red circle across my wrist. Until Daisy, a little girl we met on our walk, kept complaining about a wasp sting.

Curious to see what a sting looked like, I asked, "May I see?"

When she showed it to me, I looked at my wrist and smiled, "I've got one too."

Iris scoffed, "You'd know it if you had one, like Daisy. She's complaining because it hurts really bad. You only just said something about yours now. It can't be what it is.."

I shrugged and kept walking alongside Chris on his bike. Iris was going back home to cut a potato for Daisy's wasp sting. It was supposed to help take away the pain and swelling.

Before going inside, Iris sighed at me, "Let me see your wrist. I know what a wasp sting looks like."

I showed her my wrist, and she gasped, "We've got to take care of this immediately. The stinger is still in your wrist! That's gotta hurt."

I shrugged and calmly replied, "It's not too bad."

Chris stayed outside as Daisy and I followed Iris inside.

We got our potato slices, and I went back outside hurriedly. Daisy wanted to ensure her sting would get better, so Iris kept watching over it. I just threw the slice on my wrist and walked out the door. It didn't hurt too badly. I only said something because I thought it was nice that Daisy didn't have to be the only one that was wounded by the peach tree. I thought of it as that's what we deserved for stealing, but there were so many peaches they were falling and rotting on the ground. It was almost a crime not to take them out of the fenced-in yard if they were going to go to waste. We only took one each, after all. The universe didn't see it that way, but I accepted taking a bite from karma to enjoy the juicy, tangy peach.

When I walked down the steps of Claire's trailer, I spotted three kids surrounding Chris with his bike sitting beside him on the ground.

I stood up straight, hurrying to Chris as I yelled, "Leave him alone. He didn't do anything to you. Is it because he's cuter than you? He's my boyfriend, not yours. Leave him alone."

A chubby boy scoffed, "Oh wow. You have to let a girl fight all your battles for you? You're a wimp! I'll see you later, girly boy when your *girlfriend* isn't around anymore."

The other kids laughed and took off on their bikes.

I helped Chris from off the ground as I whispered, "I'm sorry. I just couldn't watch them pick on you. I had to protect you."

Chris smiled without smiling and asked with tears in his eyes, "How did you know they wouldn't hurt you? They kicked me to the ground."

I thought for a moment and whispered, "I didn't. I just couldn't let them bully you. I would take their punishment if it took it away from you."

He looked down towards the ground, embarrassed that he didn't stand up for himself, and smiled, "You're so brave. I wish I could be more like you."

I hugged him as I whispered in his ear, "I'm not as brave as you think I am. I never stood up for myself. Only for you."

I smiled at him as he sniffled and tried not to cry.
He cleared his throat and hurried, "I've got to go home now."

I kissed him goodbye for the night, unable to say anything to make it better.

Iris and Daisy walked out as Chris rode away on his bike. Iris asked, "What happened? Why did Chris leave? Did y'all have a fight?"
I replied, "No, nothing happened. Chris just had to go home for

some reason. It's probably dinner time."
Chris looked back at me with his brown hair in his eyes, showing he had heard me and smiled genuinely before riding away. He was dreamy even when he felt weak.

Iris invited Daisy's brother, David, to come over, so he brought his dad, Murray, who was Mom's friend, to cook for all of us. Murray began to fire up the grill on Clair's grill. I followed everyone up the stairs, wanting to see how a fire was built, until at the beginning of the porch, a five-inch nail stuck itself into the heel of my foot. I could not get free, and it hurt too much not to cry. The entire nail was stuck in my foot, which was stuck to the porch. I screamed for help. Murray came right away, forgetting all about the meat on the smoker. He hollered for David, who was alone with my cousin in her room, until he came out, straightening his clothes to look presentable.

Murray shook his head as he saw him and ordered, "Go back to the house and bring some medicine. I need monkey's blood and bandages... and some Neosporin while you're at it. Hurry, go."

Dave jogged off to their house to get the medical supplies for my wound. Murray tried to pry my foot from the nail, but it hurt too badly to allow him to get very far.

Murray hushed, "That's okay. We need the iodide to help get it out anyway, to keep off any infection or tendonitis from this rusty nail. Have you had a tetanus shot recently?"

I gasped through the pain, "I don't know. Just get it out. It hurts so bad. So bad. I just want it out."

Murray rubbed the top of my foot as we waited for David to return. Murrary cooed, "It's alright, baby doll. Just keep breathing. It'll come out soon."

David returned with the supplies a few minutes later. Murray hissed, "What took you so long, boy? Can't you see this girl needs help?"

Dave stammered, "I'm sorry, sir. I'll do better next time. It just took me…"

Murray interrupted, "That's fine boy. Just get back to whatever it is you were doing. That's what you're good at, right?"

David disappeared inside Claire's trailer.

Iodine was smothered all over my ankle. I worried about diseases I could get from having monkey's blood running through my veins. I tried not to look at the blood tincture working as a lubricant to remove the nail from the heel of my foot. I looked down to see how much of the nail had gotten into my foot once it was removed. It was a solid three inches of red-rusted metal. Murray wrapped my ankle with a cloth bandage and smiled when he was done, returning to the meat in the smoker that was luckily not burned. After dinner, Murray asked if we'd like to spend the night at his house with his kids. Iris was ecstatic because she wanted to win David over as her boyfriend, and the more time they had together might make it happen. Iris was still dating Corey but would leave him instantly for the opportunity to be with David. We sneaked back to Murray's house without telling Claire we would be gone all night. It was unlikely she would even notice as she kept herself locked in her room most days.

Daisy was friendly enough but had a strange obsession with the things that occurred under the bridge of the lake. I didn't even know what bridge she was talking about, although I had crossed the bridge in the car to get to Lewisville, where the trailer park was. I just hadn't paid attention.

Daisy jittered in whispers as if talking to herself, "…You know, S-E-X. That's where they do it. They do it. I've seen it. If you want, I can take you to the bridge, where they do it, so you can do it with Chris. Iris told me she doesn't want Chris doing what he does with other girls, but I can make it happen. You wanna go tomorrow? Do you like S-E-X?"

I had no idea what she was talking about, but I declined. Had I known, I would have refused as well. She was the same age as me, but something had corrupted her.

She breathed in a sigh of relief, "Good. You want to stay little. Little is good. I wish I were little, little like you. Stay little as long as you can. I've never been like that. I couldn't with...." She stopped mid-sentence, but her conversations were difficult to keep up with as if she were talking in riddles. She confused me. She was the same age as me and just as little.

David was a bit of a brute. I kept forgetting his name, thinking his name was Chris. The second time I called him by the wrong name, he pushed me against a wall and trapped me in a cage of his arms, bellowing, "I'm not your little boyfriend! Quit calling me by his name! If you want me to pretend to be him, I can show you, but you won't like it"

I winced, "No! I know you're not my boyfriend. You're nothing like him. I thought that was your name too."

He sighed grumpily, "I'm David. Day-vid! Don't you get it wrong again!" He slammed his fist against the wall by my face and walked away.

What my cousin saw in him was a mystery. He was rude, foul, and seemed to be abusive. I guess every girl adores a bad boy. All I saw was hideosity. I didn't speak to him after he threatened me. I tried to be friendly before, but he wasn't worth trying to be nice for. Granny always said, "If you can't say something nice, don't say anything at all."

It was time for bed, and all there was to sleep on was a queen size mattress in the corner on the floor in a small room. I looked around as if it were some sort of joke, but this is where everyone was expected to sleep. David slept in the far corner by the wall, and Iris laid cuddled next to him. Murray took a spot next to my cousin; there was only space for one tiny body in the queen-sized bed. One of us girls would have to sleep on the floor by themselves.

Murray beamed, "Which one of you lovely ladies gets the

pleasure of sleeping next to me? Why don't you race for it? ... Ready. Set. Go!"

The race was on.

Daisy pleaded, "No, no, no," as she tried to beat me to the last spot.

She even tried to cheat the race by flinging her hands in front of me, her arms flailing around helplessly to block my win. It made the victory that much sweeter.

Murray smiled, "You win! Great job. You're really fast, pretty girl."

Daisy pouted as she laid next to me on the floor, whispering, "We could just go sleep over there on the floor together if you want."

I didn't want to sleep on the floor anymore. I wanted to sleep in a bed, even if the bed was on the floor. I just wanted to be like everybody else.

I should have just slept on the floor with Daisy, but hindsight is 50/50.

Obtaining a spot on the bed wasn't a prize or something to be desired, not when it was next to Murray. It was some sick game that I could never have imagined had it not happened to me.

Daisy's beautiful soul was willing to take another night of the torture just so I could stay little. Little in the way, she never got to experience. No warning could have been said that would have gotten the point across.

Murray slowly began to transform as everyone drifted off to sleep.

I thought a bug was crawling on my leg, but when I went to scratch it, it disappeared. I felt my dress slowly crawl up my leg. I itched my leg, where I felt a possible string drag across my legs. My dress began to rise up at a quickened pace. I thought it had only moved because of some friction in the bed pulling it up. I pulled my dress down as far as it could go to remain covered. I huffed, annoyed at the discomfort that continued.

Feet padded against the floor hurriedly until reaching the

empty space in front of the closet, where Daisy had offered us both to sleep. I thought she must have felt something crawling on her as well, ants in the carpet or something of that nature. Something was unbearably itchy. I was at the end of the bed, so maybe whatever it was had crept up the mattress.

I never opened my eyes. In some way I knew there wasn't a bug moving my dress. I was just used to strange occurrences at night that I was told weren't real. This probably wasn't real, either. I was just anxious about being in new surroundings. I was discomforted sleeping next to a stranger, even if he was Mom's friend. I didn't know what it could be, but I didn't think Murray was the one pulling my dress up to get better access to what was inside.

I drifted off to sleep feeling crazy for imagining things.

When I woke up two hours later, my panties were at my ankles. My dress was pushed up to my chest, crushed into my neck. My right hand no longer belonged to me. It was molded around the private parts of Murray. He was nothing but a sick, slimy, sweat-covered worm lying next to me. The worm had dug a cavity underneath the space from where I pee. This cavity couldn't have existed before. If it did, I didn't know about it. He had dug a wormhole inside my body with his finger that inhabited it. His hand rested where my underwear should have been.

I just wanted to go back to sleep where the act never happened. I wanted to return to my locked room where no one ever looked at me. I should've asked Chris to run away with me. I chose the wrong place to sleep. Maybe Iris would wake up. Someone tell me what is going on. Is this a joke? Chris, please come find me. God, dear God, why don't you make this stop? Who invented this? How do you allow this sort of thing to happen? Why do you allow suffering? You only get what you deserve, right? Is this what I deserve? For what? What have I ever done that compares to this? Take it away! Make it stop!

I slowly began to release my grasp of the flesh I held in my unconsenting hand. I didn't want him to know I was awake.

I just wanted it to stop and pretend it never happened. His hand incessantly reassured my grasp, gripping it harder than before. I constricted my grasp even harder, hoping it would hurt so he would take it away. He let out a gasp of enjoyment instead. I let go again, getting a little further away than before. He replaced my hand into a vice once more. I placed my hand firmly at my side. He huffed in disappointment.

His finger wiggled in my dry wormhole as pleasure was deprived from his slithering body. My stomach churned in an upheaval of disgust. I could feel my insides being punctured. My stomach decayed with his slimy touch. I tried once more to find a hero in the chaos. I thought of my star. I pictured the dark sky above and called out to my twinkling star.

She answered immediately. *Oh, my dear, Annie, what can I do to help*? I pleaded in silence, *Make it stop, please. Just make it stop. Take it away. Make it all just go away. Why does this exist? Who does this? Can you make it never happen? Take it back, please. Take it away. Take me away from here now.* It hushed, *My darling if only I could. I can't make any part of this better. I can't undo what the world has done. I don't have that power. I'm not magic. You have to get yourself out of this. You have to open your eyes.* Hot tears poured out of my shut eyes. I whined. *I can't. I just can't. I don't want to. I don't want to be here. Take it away. Please.* It hummed, *My Annie. My dear Storm, I can't. Only you can do this. You can do this. Open your eyes and see. Please, Annie. Trust me. I'd never steer you wrong. Open your eyes. Just open your eyes and see. I'll be with you the whole time.*

I turned my head to the disgusting worm and opened my eyes to stare into the eyes of the worm. The star spoke through me, "What are you doing?"

He laid there naked, completely exposed, his body laying as straight as possible, stretched out, precisely like a grub worm. As soon as I spoke, his finger was removed from within me. He jolted up, grabbing up his clothes scattered all across the bed, next to my cousin and his sleeping son. Daisy was no longer in the room. I pulled up my panties and pulled down my dress. I followed the scrambling worm into the next room. He zipped around the kitchen, ensuring he stayed across the room from me. He looked terrified.

Good.

He sputtered, "Please, Annie, I just don't... I can't... I just can't right now. I can't go through this right now. Please."

Murray tripped over his pants as he attempted to put them on while getting tangled in his shirt as well. He couldn't stand still as he struggled to dress himself. I took a step closer to him, bathing in his fear.

I repeated, "What did you just do to me? What were you thinking?"

I felt like a tiger, ready to pounce on my victim, to tear off his head, separate the skin from his body. He was just a worm. Why not? Nobody could miss him. Nobody could know what he was. I'd be doing the world a favor if I dragged his body to the lake, inside the boathouse. If I just pulled him into the canoe and dropped him halfway through the lake and let the gars dispose of his body.

I asked, "Why me? Is that what you do to Daisy? Do you think she likes that? Nobody does. That was the most..."

He cut me off, looking me in the eyes with his arms out and wrist wiggling back and forth to signal

"Stop," he pleaded, "Please just forgive me."

"Oh..." he yowled, "Oh... God, your mother. Your mother would never forgive me. Please... just don't tell anyone. Don't tell your mom, please. She'll never..."

He started to cry and rushed out the door. The feeling of the star's empowerment left me as he closed the door, and I sank back into the events that had just taken place.

What should I do? What can I do?

I walked back into the dark room. Daisy laid asleep in the corner by the door. She wasn't there before. I whispered, "Iris, Iris. Pst... Wake up! Iris!" She laid asleep and had dozed through it all.

Daisy had woken up, but what could she do? She couldn't stop or watch it happen, as she must have felt powerless and afraid.

I hope she got to listen to him beg.

I couldn't leave without Iris, so I laid on the floor by the bed and fell asleep, trying to wait for Iris to wake up. I woke up again, sleeping next to Daisy, when Iris shook me and hissed, "We have to get home before Mom wakes up and knows we've been gone."

For the first time this week, I didn't think of Chris as I woke up. I didn't think of anyone except God, and how I didn't believe he existed anymore. The only God was the star. Even if there was a God, he couldn't be bothered to respond. I secured my faith in the stars and the universe. What happened couldn't be undone, but it gave me the courage to end the nightmare of the worm.

All the freedom and happiness I had found this week was turned to ash after this event. Falling in love faded away. When I saw Chris again, I smiled, but it wasn't the same as before.

When we got back to Iris's house, Claire slurred, "...Where you whores ran off to? Y'all been spreadin' your legs all over town, I bet, gone all night. Babies make babies running around all hours of the night. Did ya think I wouldn't find out? I know... I know everything."

Iris put Claire in her room. Iris and I went back to our room to try to plan how to make my mom let me stay with Iris so I could become her sister. Iris had always wanted a sister and felt it should be me. I enjoyed Iris's company, although I dreaded a future sleepover if she wanted to be with David again. Also, I didn't know what I could say to Daisy if I saw her again.

Do I say sorry for her having such a perverse father that probably touches her at night? Can I ask why she kept moving around the room as her dad touched me? Or do I act like it never happened? The right way to speak to her was lost on me as I knew she was the only one that knew what had happened to me.

Later that day, Daisy came over to ask me a question. She requested quietly, "Can I talk to Annie alone?"

Iris replied hesitantly, "Sure."

She left the room, leaving Daisy and me together. My palms sweat. I didn't know what to say, what to do, or how to even be in a room with her while we were both keeping secrets that were too terrible to say out loud.

After a few minutes of silence, Daisy asked, "So there's this dance coming up at school. I don't have a date, but since you're leaving, I was thinking... Would you mind if I went to the dance with Chris and took him as my boyfriend?

My face had to have turned beet red as my jaw dropped to the floor. She wanted my Chris? But he's mine, and I love him. I'm leaving, though, so maybe I should let him go. I should allow him to move on, to forget me... But I didn't want him to forget me. I wanted him to remember me for years to come, for him to feel as I felt... That no matter the distance, he had my heart. He was mine, and I was his. Distance can't stop that. But I should allow him closure. He deserved someone to be there for him. The thought of it, though was not something I could accept or cope with. I wanted him. He chose me, not her. She had been living in the trailer park for years, unnoticed by him. I was the thing that made her notice him. It's not fair! She deserves to be happy. To have someone she wants to touch her instead of all of the repulsive nights she had to have had, waking up to her father molesting her. She asked for my permission out of respect for me. My answer probably didn't matter anyway. I'm just going to say how I feel.

After a long pause after her question, I replied, "No. He's my boyfriend. He shouldn't go on dates with you. You're great and all but... I can't say yes with the thoughts of picturing the two of you. I love him so much, so it's a no from me. But you can ask him. Whatever he says is fine with me. I just don't want to know."

Daisy nodded, soaking in my words, and began to walk away. She turned around as she reached the bedroom door and whispered, "I'm sorry for what Daddy did to you. He does it to me too."

My eyes watered up with tears as I replied, "I know. It was me or you last night.."

She whimpered, "Yeah...but I really tried to save you."

I nodded as I cried, "I know, but I was too stubborn."

Daisy nodded as she said, "Bye." and left the trailer.

Daisy walked in and worried, "Are you okay? What did she say?"

I scrubbed my face with my hands, trying to remove the tears covering my face.

I replied, "Nothing."

Iris insisted, "It wasn't nothing. What did she say? You better tell me. I'm your friend."

I nodded, "Okay. She just... She asked me if Chris could go to the dance with her since I'm being taken away."

Iris hummed, "Ohhh, I see. What'd you say? You said yes, right?"

I shook my head as I whimpered, "No, I just couldn't. It would've been the right thing to do, but I couldn't stand the thought of it."

Iris retorted, "You should have said yes. As much as I want you to stay, you're probably leaving today."

I sighed, "I told her to ask Chris, and if he said yes, they can do whatever they want. I just don't want to know."

Iris nodded as she looked out the window through the blinds.

Iris gasped, "Your mom's here! I've got to get Chris!"

Iris met Mom at the front door and greeted her as she brushed by her, saying, "Hello, Auntie. I was just going out for a sec, but I'll be right back. It's good to see you. Mom's in her room in the back if you want to visit with her for a while."

Mom walked towards Clair's door and knocked to talk to her for a bit since she hadn't spent enough time to be able to chat with her when I was dropped off. I stayed in Iris's room until she came back with Chris.

Chris looked at me with wide, puppy-dog eyes and said, "So you're about to leave I guess. That's what Iris said."

I mumbled, "Yeah. My Mom is here to take me with her, I guess. I really don't want to go. I love you. You are the sweetest boy on the planet. I wish I could be with you all the time. You mean a lot to me. This week has been the best week of my life, and I'm so glad I got to spend it with you."

Chris smiled brightly as his face moved towards mine, and we kissed as grown-ups do to make up for all the time we wouldn't have together. I tried not to cry as he held my hand as we sat on the bed, unable to come up with any words to say with my imminent departure.

Iris looked at us with teary eyes and beamed, "You guys are so cute together! It's like the perfect love story... Okay, look, I have the plan to get you to stay, but you have to do as I say, got it?"

Chris and I both nodded our heads and said yes.

Iris began, "So I want you two to go in there where our moms are talking, and I want you to kiss. Kiss as many times as you can. Profess your love to one another loudly. Make sure they see you. If they're not paying attention, it won't work, so make sure to grab their attention. That's it. That's all I've got to get you to stay. If they see how deeply you two are in love, then there's no way she'd take you away. You got this."

Chris and I stood up and walked down the hall into the living room slowly, unsure how Iris's plan would work and not really wanting to make out in front of my mom. Iris gently pushed us into the living room as she whispered, "Go!"

Chris and I held hands and walked across the living room as if we were on a runway together and kissed right next to Mom as we said I love you and continued holding hands all the way back to the sanctuary of the hall.

Iris hissed, "Go do it again, but bigger, better. Show them how much you really care for one another."

I replied. "Okay." I looked at Chris and inhaled sharply, "You ready?

He nodded, and we walked into the living room, holding hands skipping gleefully until reaching the end of the kitchen, where we kissed as we had on Iris's bed. Mom glared with a confused expression on her face until looking back at my aunt sitting next to her at the kitchen table. We walked closer to the kitchen table, and I blared, "I don't know what I'd do without your love, Chris. You are the man of my dreams!"

I grabbed him by his face and kissed him as hard as possible, trying to show Mom I didn't want to leave.

Mom paused and trumpeted, "Annie! What are you doing with that boy? Is this what you've been up to the whole time?"

Chris walked to Iris into the safety of the hallway. He didn't know what to do as he watched me be scolded.

I replied, "Not all the time, but I like spending time with Chris. He's my boyfriend. I don't wanna go. I want to stay here with Iris and live happily ever after."

Mom scoffed, "Yeah…that's definitely not happening. You're not old enough to decide on your own."

I looked back at Chris as he was unable to hide his tears as he escaped through the front door. He couldn't say goodbye. We shouldn't have to. We didn't do anything wrong. Mom didn't really want me, so what was the problem?

I stomped my foot angrily as I pouted, "You don't love me or even want me. You just keep me to hold me prisoner and watch Orion because you don't want to. Iris takes good care of me, and I just want to stay in love and sleep in a real bed. I didn't do anything wrong.'

Claire sirened, "That's your Mom. She brought you into this world, and she can take you out just as easily. Parents have that right."

Mom smiled as she agreed, "That's right. So stop whining and get your things together. I have a surprise for you. We're going to be on a road trip for a while, but I didn't forget, it's your birthday! We'll go out to eat and celebrate your day as long as you're good."

I sighed, "Okay… but if you leave me here, you don't have

to surprise me. I'll be happy enough."

Mom barked, "You are not staying here a moment longer. Now get your things and get in the car."

I walked to the hall with my head down. I forgot today was my birthday. I turned eight years old. The first gift I received was Murray touching me and making me touch his in return. *Happy Birthday!*

I kissed Chris an infinite amount of times, and that was the best present I could receive, besides being allowed to say here. *I'm just going to be trapped again. I just know it!* Without being granted my wish, any surprise I could be given was certain to pale in comparison.

Iris whispered, "Sorry, Annie. I really thought that would work."

I sighed, "I know. It was worth a try."

I collected all of my clothes from Iris's bedroom floor and shoved them in a trash bag, and took it outside to go in the car. Chris was standing at the side of the house, waiting for me to come out. I dropped my bag and jumped into his arms. I kissed him as he held my waist in his arms, holding me close. He said, "I will never forget you. I love you. Just to let you know, Daisy asked me to the school dance, and I said yes. You wouldn't be able to go to the school dance anyway since you don't attend our school. Are you mad?"

I stared at the ground and said, "No, I'm not mad. You're right. I wouldn't be able to go either way. I hope you have fun."

Mom walked outside when she was ready to go and got in her car. I picked up my bag and waved bye to Chris one last time. He began to walk back home, as there was no way to make this have a good ending. Maybe if I were kinder or less possessive, but it's part of who I am and how I love.

Iris rushed out of the trailer as I opened the car door and threw my bag in the backseat. Iris hugged me and picked me up in her arms, exclaiming, "I'm going to miss you, little cuz. I had so much fun having you as a sister for a week."

I smiled, "Me too. Thank you for everything."

Iris hugged me again and went back inside. I sat down beside my bag and closed the car door.

Mom began to drive off as she berated, "What were you doing kissing that boy so many times. Once, I can understand, but as many as that… look at your lip. That's what happens with boys like that. Kissing a boy like that will make you have cold sores. Once you have them, the virus lives inside you for life. It's disgusting. What made you think I'd let you stay there? I can't believe your cousin or my sister for that matter. They've just been letting you run wild. That's what happens. Give you an inch, and you take a mile."

Mom's words hurt, but not as much as the hollow hole inside of my stomach, ripping through my intestines like tiny daggers. It had started last night, but the knives were getting sharper and faster now as the hollow nothing took over my body. A giant piece of me had been taken away. I hadn't had time to process the occurrence of last night. It was flooding my brain now. That and all of the negative experiences from yesterday to today. The sky turned into black ash instead of a cloudy blue sky with a warm sun. Everything was gray and covered in the tar of inescapable shadow.

7. The Drooling Spider

Home was now an RV, or would be once we traveled to Georgia. Mom was given a job opportunity to manage a coffee shop there and couldn't turn down the opportunity. As we made our way out of Texas, our tiny new home traveled behind Rob's black truck.

For my birthday, I really wanted to not be called Annie anymore. Annie died at the hands of the worm because she never woke up. I was the creation that came afterward and I could endure the pain for her. My official reason was I just wanted to go by my actual name. It seemed easier on my mind to put away everything that had happened to Annie. I wanted a fresh start, hoping things would improve in our new home. I had been gone for a week, and apparently, Mom had to have me back, so maybe she missed me while I was gone. Things could only get better, right?

The trip from Texas to Georgia was long. I didn't understand why we traveled north of Texas just to head east, but I wasn't the navigator. All of us slept in the truck, but ate at many different restaurants along the way. I didn't know different states had different restaurants I had never heard of before. A place called 'Ole Folks seemed to be the family favorite. There were even miniature wooden peg boards at each table for Orion and me to play with while we waited for our meals.

Orion was a good travel companion. He was three years old and just beginning to talk, fluent in his secret language. Most of what he said was, *"Tika, ticka,"* the only thing that made it its own language was the *'ticka'* changed pace and order. Sometimes it was more of a *'tick-tick-tick-ah.'* Or if he was angry, it came out *'tictickatickatickatick-ah.'* The game for the road trip Orion and I invented was called, *'Ahh-No!'* Which was said right before a slap to the thigh, which Orion absolutely adored. The harder I slapped his leg, the louder he would giggle. His giggle made me laugh, so the trip was spent in slaps and giggles until we arrived in the middle of Georgia.

We stayed in an RV lot that was much like a trailer park, only the homes were substantially smaller. Mom and Rob had an upstairs loft with a memory foam mattress in the RV. Orion and I slept on a hard bench of the square kitchen table that was supposed to double as a bed, but it was worse than sleeping on the floor. It was exquisitely uncomfortable. Orion often slept in bed with mom and Rob so I could 'have more room'. He only slept with me on the days they wanted to have sex, and he wouldn't go to sleep.

I was never invited into the loft and was told to never enter the area for any reason, even if there was a fire. They were to never be disturbed.

I stayed on the square bench without a level middle, squished between the sharply cornered table and the hard backside of the hard seats.

Have you ever tried sleeping on a park bench, or on the seat of one of the picnic tables? It was like that, only hardwood instead of plastic. The table was closer than it should have been. Rob couldn't even sit at it because his belly was too big. Sleeping was excruciatingly painful. If you jerked just right, you could hit your head in a sharp corner and be told to go back to sleep. So you do, while crying because there's a bleeding wound on your face from where it hit the wood. Don't cry too loud, though; then you'll be given something 'to cry about.' I wasn't sure what that was. I just covered my face securely in the sheet to try to muffle the sound. Nobody cared if I was hurt. Why did my face bother to cry? That's what you get for existing.

I HATED this place. I wasn't wanted. I just wouldn't be

given to someone that didn't bear the torture of giving birth to me, especially not to 'trailer trash'. I was Mom's child to ignore, nobody else's, except for Rob... but I declined being ANYTHING of his. My suffering was all his doing. Mom was just an accomplice or an enabler... or she didn't care. Pick one. Any of them is the right answer. It doesn't matter anyways.

Heavy smoke would fill the RV at night, and if I coughed, Rob would snicker, "Well, your mom likes it. Talk to her if you want me to stop." Mom would giggle and begin whispering in Rob's ear.

Being comfortable any part of the day was against the rules. My life consisted of being shoved in places I didn't fit and negged into obedience.

I went back to school starting in the third grade. I was told I was homeschooled throughout the second grade. *I guess the siren babysitter had been a teacher as well. What an interesting piece of plastic.*

I learned from second grade what it feels like to live in solitary confinement, although at least in prison, they have access to a toilet.

I made one friend at the school in Georgia. She was a kind, chubby-cheeked girl with dark skin and a bright spirit. My name was too weird to fit in with the rest of the kids, and my voice didn't speak as the people in Georgia spoke. That didn't matter to Quinta. She had the same issues trying to fit in but had an added issue of being a different race than the rest of the class and perhaps anyone at all in the school. Her skin was like velvety dark chocolate. Quinta smiled out of joy more often than anyone else I saw. We spent all of our recesses and lunches together, so neither of us had to be alone.

On the bus, I made friends with a first grader sitting behind me who tapped me on the shoulder and asked if I could come over to ride bikes together. I said yes, even though I was unsure if she truly wanted to hang out with me. I asked for permission to hang out with someone that might be my friend and was allowed as long as I was home before dark. I walked through the RV park to her beautiful home at the top of the hill. I hadn't caught the little girl's name, so it was a bit embarrassing when her parents answered the door and asked who I was looking for. I tried to describe her until her dad asked if I was looking for the big or mini version. She gleefully smiled when she came to the door and took my hand to show me outside where the bikes were. She rode a bike without training wheels, and I had to admit, I don't know how to ride a bike without the two little back wheels that kept a bike balanced.

She smiled, "I'll teach you. Easy-peasy."

This little girl was an excellent teacher, full of patience and encouragement. I spent every day after school with the angel in first grade and learned to ride a *real* bike in a week. We rode her bikes through the woods surrounding her house and always had fun together. Nobody else was ever at her house besides her family. I'm not sure what made her choose me, but I was thankful she had. She had been an excellent friend and teacher, but I never could remember her name.

My family moved back to Texas in a one-bedroom house owned by Rob's mom. Orion and I had the bedroom in the back of the house by the bathroom. Mom and Rob used the office area of the house as their bedroom which separated the living room from ours. I was surprised by being given the large room, but Mom said, "You're both getting bigger now. You need more space."

It actually made sense after the house was set up with our belongings. Mom and Rob didn't want to have to walk through our room all of the time and have to see children. The only downside to this setup was we had to walk through their room to get to the kitchen. There were no locks placed on the doors. They couldn't implant the siren box because who wants to unlock it every time you need to run to the bathroom? It's all a matter of convenience. The door separating our rooms eventually broke anyway, so a sheet was set up to cover the doorframe, so afterwards the door was thrown away. Our door was taken off to try to replace the broken one, but it was too difficult to place, so that door disappeared too. Somehow it was our fault; something about being too hard on the door we barely had a chance to touch. Maybe it was a joke, but I didn't find it funny.

I walked into their room to go to the kitchen to make Orion and me dinner.

Mom squawked dramatically, "I should have never had children! You were a mistake! If I could take it all back, I would. Believe me, I would take you back in a heartbeat! You kids are going to be the death of me! Why?!" Mom threw herself onto her bed, lying face down, bawling. I was in shock as I stood speechless. I couldn't even be offended as all I was trying to do was walk to the kitchen to cook for my brother like the responsible adult I wasn't.

Rob walked into the room from the living room. For a second, I thought he might correct her or say that she was being cruel, but instead, Rob snickered and pushed me off to my room.

He exclaimed, "I'm about to have sex with your mother! I am going to destroy her in a way that has never been done before. She's gonna love it! If you don't want to see my big cock penetrating her, I suggest you go back to your room and hide under the covers."

Mom giggled excitedly as I stumbled into the safety of the hall. Rob's belt was undone, and his pants were coming off before I could fully get past the sheet door. He wasn't wearing any underwear, but I began to run back to my room.

After coming to the room, I told Orion, "I'm sorry, I'll have to feed you later. We can't go out for now." He looked quizzically at the missing door, and I shook my head to signify no. He nodded in understanding, or at least accepted my answer, and proceeded to watch TV. I turned the volume of our boxy television up as loud as it would go as I tried to muffle the groans occuring in the next room as we watched *Teenage Mutant Ninja Turtles* together. We went to bed without dinner.

After settling in, Mom was rarely home. She began waitressing at *IHOP*, often working both mornings and nights. The time she spent at home was a period of hibernation. No one was to disturb her or play too loud. As long as Orion and I were quiet, we could do what we liked.

The grown-ups rarely ate at home. Occasionally one of them would cook, but that involved a family dinner where we were expected to sit still, display manners, and socialize with the adults. It hardly seemed worth it. Mostly when these events occurred, Rob informed me, "No one is going to want to marry or date you when you eat like that. You need to learn table manners and how to take smaller bites. Smaller portions even. Nobody wants to see you eat and make a mess of yourself." I did the best I could to be civilized, but it never seemed good enough to be anything anyone would ever want to be around.

At a family brunch, Rob announced, "We are going to initialize a family decree. We are all to become nudists, which means no one is to be constricted to clothing. It's an order! Let it all come off. Let the bodies be freed." On that note, he unbuttoned his shirt and threw it into his chair dramatically. He paused for applause. With his shaggy torso exposed, his round belly floundered as he breathed heavily.

I continued scraping my food from one side of the plate to the other. Orion looked at me with wide blue eyes and waited for instruction. I raised an eyebrow as I took an undesired bite of the scrambled eggs and shrugged.

Rob bellowed, "There will be no insubordination here! This is an order! Do you know what order means?"

I gazed at him quizzically.

I stood up and helped Orion from his chair as I hushed, "Come on, buddy, let's go to our room."

Rob gruffed, "You are not excused!"

I smiled, "I don't have to do anything you tell me. I'm not your dog."

I never pretended to be nice to him.

The ghost of Mom breathed as she took Rob's arm, "Just let them go. They're done eating."

Rob stepped away from Mom as we walked through the living room. He shouted, "You do have to do what I tell you, little girl. I'm the master. You're all my little slaves, and this is my house. You will obey me under my roof! ...Fine, that's just fine. Run along, little slaves. You are dismissed from your master."

As we walked through Mom's room in hushed tones, I heard Rob say, "Don't you ever interrupt me again."

Mom hummed, "Yes, master."

I couldn't make Orion wear clothes. Even though I dressed as usual, he wanted to do what he was told.

I tried to ignore the odd behaviors around the house.

Luckily, all underwear remained on in the nudist colony. Orion drew family portraits of stick figures with hairy pubic mounds accompanied by squiggly smell lines. *Did private parts smell bad? What went on when I went to school?*

The second half of third grade was strange. For the very first time, I wasn't an outcast. Every day the same boy would attempt to serenade me during lunch. Instead of eating his meal, he sang, "Oh Storm, oh Storm, oh beautiful Storm. When will we set the date?" Sammy, a beautiful Latina girl with big brown eyes, decided that we were to be best friends and invited me over to her house after school. She lived right across the street from me, so I was allowed to spend most days after school at her home.

Her mom, Linda, was wonderfully friendly and constantly present. She had dark pixie-cut hair with perfectly placed bleached tips. Her skin had a stunning caramel glow, and her plump lips were tattooed with maroon lip liner around the edges to make them look even bigger than they were. She welcomed me into her home with open arms, often offering us homemade meals she cooked or something from the popsicle cart when she heard the bell ring outside. It was relieving to be able to be a kid in the presence of a loving mom. She reminded me of the mom I had when I was three. Sammy found her to be suffocating, but all I saw was love.

On the weekends, I wasn't allowed to leave the house. Mom and Rob would go out and leave me there to watch over Orion. My reward for babysitting was spending time with Sammy. That was until Rob got a job as a bail bondsman, so I was expected to be home unless I was excused to go out, which I rarely was.

I had already been watching Orion since he was a year old and feeding him, putting him to bed, and changing his diapers, so nothing changed except we had full reign of the house. We watched movies in the living room and watched television while we ate. That was all we did with freedom.

Sammy offered to come over to my house. I declined, not wanting her to see how we lived. There was no way she would ever see me the same after seeing how things worked here.

I preferred the way I was seen at school. It felt like my beauty had power, that a creature like me could even be pretty. I felt like a distortion of a person, a collage of broken parts in the mirror. I was a discarded creation of human skin made to do all the jobs no one else wanted to do. Being at school made me feel like a person as long as no mirrors were around.

When summer began, I lost my grip on my humanity and was reminded once again that I was a creation, not a living being. Attempts to reset my malfunctions began.

The first step of summer was buzz cuts for Orion and me. Our heads were ridden with lice all year, which never seemed to disappear. The easiest solution was to remove the hair that they continually infested.

Orion called our lice "Bugs Life," which was the most positive spin you could put on a head ridden with lice.

I was a bald nine-year-old girl by the time it was through. My golden blonde hair fell to the floor in long silky strands.

Mom cried, "I am so sorry, baby girl. You were so pretty. I mean, you'll still be pretty. It just won't be… the same kind of pretty as before. Luckily you have a beautiful personality."

My old habits of cheering her up remained in full swing.

I whispered, "It doesn't matter. It's okay."

I didn't cry until Mom left the room, and I looked in the mirror and thought of my fan club at school. It just won't be the same going back. A single tear fell as I looked in the mirror.

I never thought I was pretty anyway. It doesn't matter.

My hair still wasn't short enough to keep the lice from crawling, so my head was shaved to the scalp with a straight razor and covered in liquid bleach to ensure no bugs would be crawling again. The bleach burned almost more than I could bare as I tried my best not to claw at my scalp. Mom went outside for ten minutes as I suffered the itching, desperate crawling of bugs, and burning of the bleach saturating the wounds from lice bites. She came back in and said, "Good girl." She walked me over to the tub and washed my scalp with bar soap to cleanse the bleach burn away. It was the most attention I had gotten from her in a long time. It was unfortunate that it wasn't more pleasant.

Rob would come home from work periodically to check in on Orion and me. What he really did was try to convert me to be a nudist with the rest of the family. It was a royal decree, after all. It didn't help that I told him I didn't have to do anything he ever said.

My conversion consisted of a full-length mirror in the living room, the separating door to their room closed, so I would be trapped with him. If I tried to run, he'd hold my wrist in his hands and pick me up by them. He barked, "Are you going to behave?"

My answer constantly changed.

Initially, I began to uncontrollably laugh. In between laughs, I sputtered the word "No."

Rob huffed, repeating, "No?"

He stripped my clothes off aggressively, ripping them at the seams.

He bellowed, "This is what no gets you, little girl!"

My naked body dangled in front of me, reflected in the mirror. I shut my eyes, laughing so hard I cried. I pretended like this wasn't happening.

He growled through his teeth, "Open your fucking eyes, you little bitch."

Rob's hands on my wrist became rigid, somehow getting thinner, as if I were being held up by thorns. My neck became wet as he spat out ugly words. What was this liquid collecting on my neck? A thick mucus had formed. His husky body became fuzzy and bulbous, mutated to become infested with sharp pine needles.

I opened my eyes and looked at the monster behind me. He transformed into a gigantic, drooling Huntsman spider.

Vomit began to build up in my throat. My stomach couldn't handle anything that was happening. I gagged back the excrement, and the spider dropped me to the floor. The nausea fell with my body, pushing my vomit back down to my stomach.

As I gagged a final time, my fit of laughter rebooted. Rob stomped out the front door and drove away. I put my tattered clothes back on.

Despite never quite knowing what my reaction would be besides negative, Rob kept his weekly check-ins.

The second time I didn't begin my nervous laugh at first. It was only at the end when he thought I just might behave. He held my wrists in a vice in his hands and slowly pulled down my underwear with his other hand, and told me to open my eyes. When I complied, he began to chant a string of compliments.

He spat hot spider breath against my neck and growled, "You're so beautiful. Look at you. Look at your blossoming body transforming into a woman. Those hips. Mmm. You could be growing hair down there soon. Your body is perfect. Don't you want to show it off? Make me happy and show it off. You don't even need to wear panties. Show me how pretty you are. You're stunning, little girl. Do as the master says. I want to watch you grow."

The laughing fit began again as I uttered the word no. I guess he enjoyed a challenge.

A man with a God complex does not like being told no. He had a significant case of "Little Big Man Syndrome", and a nine-year-old girl was making him feel very small. The last time it occurred, he only had to hold my wrist to make me look at myself. I eventually gave in, at least saying yes. Upon this response, the spider hissed, "Did you mean yes, Sir?" I smiled, holding the last morsel of rebellion, "No."

Fourth grade came, which should have been my escape from home. The only upside was I could wear clothes. I had been walking around in my underwear for far too long. My hair had only grown an inch since it was shaved. I was a stranger in a foreign yet familiar world.

All of the kids gawked uncomfortably, even while walking Orion to his first day at school.

I was asked if we were twins or if he was just shorter than me. The trending question was if I was a boy or a girl. Everyone *had* to know.

My classmates from last year didn't recognize me. After telling them my name was Storm, they began to laugh. My entire existence was a mockery. Sammie was no longer my friend. To be her friend, you had to be pretty. Otherwise, you were just one of her minions that delivered messages. I wouldn't be talked down to or be anyone's slave. For that reason, we got into many fights that year without speaking to one another.

I spent my days in class in the back corner where no one would notice me.

For the next summer, Rob declared, "Your job for the summer, little girl, is manual labor. Do you know how to define manual labor? It means hard work and sweat. You have to earn your rewards. I need a hole dug 6 feet deep by the side of the house, going four feet wide under the house.

I objected, "Why?"

He scoffed, "You're not supposed to argue, little girl. Just say yes, master, and get it done. I'll make it worth your while."

I rolled my eyes and ignored the request for two weeks until I grew complacent. I could go outside and not be restricted to staying in that house watching Orion.

I was growing weary of listening to his strange hums and explosions of *'I'm a genius!'* as he drew stick figures of the family and Sonic naked with bushes and stink lines. *You're disturbing is what you are*, I thought.

He can't help it, stop it, I said to myself. The day I shouted, "You're not a genius! I can do so many more things than you! I draw better. My homework is stuff you can't even compute. So stop saying you're a genius when you're not! And stop drawing everything naked!"

I needed some air. I wasn't meant to be a caretaker this young. I tried to never be rude to anyone, especially Orion. I was exhausted by nothing ever going my way, being stuck with nowhere to go, and Orion's sudden vocal explosions were a bit much. It didn't matter what he said or did. It wasn't about that. It was more about me and being stuck thinking with no foreseeable way out. I felt imprisoned everywhere I went. Maybe I could feel free outside.

Logically, one could say I could have run away. I could have stolen some money and just disappeared. I thought about it, but I didn't know where to go. I didn't know if it would be any better or if all places and homes were equally as bad as it was here. I was just growing older, and that's what happens. At least I lived with a thermostat and had food to eat, and could try to keep the negativity away from Orion the majority of the time. I was used to it. I could handle it better. He wasn't a baby anymore, so attention was no longer positive. It only gets worse as you age. What would make any other place better? I only wished someone would ask me to run away with them. I was terrified of being alone.

Initially, digging the hole felt a lot like obeying the spider. I paused as I thought about it… he wanted his hole dug two weeks ago. I never had the intention of doing it because he wanted it complete. It was only when I needed something to relieve the stress that made me feel like I was on the verge of my brain soldering itself to my skull.

On the first day, my hands blistered, leaving boils on both of my hands from the wooden shovel sliding back and forth against the soft flesh of my palms. It didn't keep me from digging, nor was the summer heat over a hundred degrees outside. If I kept digging, then eventually, I might be out of the sun and in the shade of the dirt hole.

Mom came outside after work, looking for me since Orion was running wild in the house.

Sweat was pouring down my face. My skin turned beet red from the sun. I was punishing myself for being rude to Orion and for staying here, for my brain being so agitated it felt like it was melting. I felt out of place with my thoughts on overdrive, tearing invisible holes within my soul. I could burn externally with my internal self to feel more symmetric.

Mom coddled, "Come inside, Storm. You've done enough for now."

I brushed the sweat from my brow and licked the salt sediment from my lips. For all my labor, all that had been dug was a pothole 4 feet long and maybe half a foot deep. It felt like I had been out in the sun for hours.

I wasn't sure how long it had actually been. I dropped the shovel to the ground and followed Mom inside.

Looking me over, she winced, "Go take a shower, and I'll

fix you right up."

I turned the water on hot and felt like I was liquifying painfully. I took a cold shower instead to wash away the fire I was becoming.

Mom put aloe vera on my inflamed skin and blistered hands. My skin felt like the fire inside my body had burned up my flesh instead of the sun. When she finished, she cooed, "Honey, stop for a week. I'll talk to master and make him ease up." I forced a smile, thanked her, and went to my room. I didn't have anything nice to say when she mentioned Rob's name.

Mom bought me a pair of rubber gloves to use the next time I felt like digging.

With the expectation to work, I halted the progression for an additional two weeks until I thought nobody expected me to try.

I dug as deep as I could in a one-session six-hour period. Rob came home from work and checked on my progress, presumably to do one of the summer check-ins he enjoyed so much. But I was outside in a hole deeper than I was tall. He stood beside the hole, switching his weight back and forth from one leg to the other. I didn't look over at him but could see him in my peripherals as I continued my work while ignoring his presence.

Rob bellowed as I pretended he wasn't standing there awkwardly, "OK, well, that's far enough... too far, actually. Why don't you start digging wide, under the house?"

I sighed, immune to heat and exhaustion, as I had been in my own world. Anything the parasite said, I felt an unyielding urge to do the opposite.

I hadn't heard his tan station wagon start-up, signaling he had left, so for once, I did what he said for another hour until I was confident he was no longer home.

I never dug again.

Rob had to finish it a week later, complaining and grunting the entire time, but he only had to continue my work for an hour until he was finished with whatever task he had in mind.

He came up to me and barked, "See how fast I got that done? If you had just tried and not sat on your lazy ass, you might've been rewarded for it."

I never found out what the hole was for, just that it was my job to fill in the seemingly pointless gutter. I declined.

Whatever 'reward' there was if it even existed, I didn't want it. I didn't want anything from him. He filled in the hole a week later.

Rob called me into the kitchen when he was finished, covered in sweat, and asked me to sit down.

Rob boomed, "Well, I was going to let you go to this when you finished. You already missed one you could have gone to, but you're terrible at listening."

I shrugged. I didn't know what he was talking about. He handed me a flier for an overnight lock-in skate party at the roller rink.

I read the paper, placed it on the table, and said, "Well, that's cool. Too bad I didn't go."

I didn't know how to skate, so I didn't care as much about this event as he thought I would. I didn't work on his timetable... I didn't care what he wanted. I was determined to do the opposite, if only for the fact that it was something he wanted. I was supposed to be broken by now... but I wasn't. That was part of his plan, too, and I was too stubborn to allow him to control me like that.

I only ever got to go to Sammie's house across the street because it had been so close, and she wasn't my friend and more. I didn't expect to get any sense of freedom again. I was a maid, a babysitter, a cook, a laundromat, manual laborer, but I unpaid for all of it. There was never a reward. It was a weak attempt to get me to do what he said more.

Little did he know I had my own reward system. I enjoyed taking things from his room when nobody was home. Nobody but Orion and I were ever home. I stole when they went on dates at night. When I felt like the only adult in the house. When they had a slew of new things with nothing for either of us. While they were at work. When he asked me to do something. When I heard any version of

Rob's name. Truly, I did every chance I could. But slowly, never much at a time, because I didn't want to be caught. I simply wanted to have a sense of control.

I stole because I was angry at the world, trapped in a life I resented. I took pieces of his Irisgraphy pen sets on the bookcase that doubled as a privacy wall in their room. There were lines of metal racks to form an extra wall in their room, filled with different collections of bins on the shelves. I liked going through the cases on the wall, taking something from each container, and destroying the complete set of everything. There were expensive pens, Indian ink, jewelry, different kinds of cigars, tobacco pipes, CDs, sex toys, you name it. I didn't care what the items were. I never used one of his pens or wore any jewelry I took. It wasn't about anything except a constant act of defiance. It was revenge, my continuous taking as I felt he took from me. I never spent the money or smoked. I was only obsessed with his tobacco products because he would chain smoke while on the toilet for an hour, pooping and smoking incessantly. We were told to use a towel if one of us needed to use the toilet. The smell of shit would've been better than all the heavy smoke that saturated the air. Even worse, after he was done, he would use an entire can of Lysol, spraying the bathroom with a white cloud of disinfectant leading out of the bathroom, encompassing the hall, and often wafting into our room. The stench of disinfectant took over, causing me to feel as though I couldn't breathe for another hour until the stench wore off. I loathed cigarettes. I loathed Lysol more. There was too much of both to be able to stomach either. It was revenge, my continuous taking as I felt he took from me. My hate for him burned like an eternal furnace. Everything he did, I loathed. I had zoned out in my thoughts. My indifference was mistaken for disappointment.

Rob tilted his head, trying to regain my attention, and continued, "But your mother and I talked about it. Since you made an effort and dug most of the hole outside, we'll let you go to the next one. It's in three days."

Was this some trick? I felt confused and surprised. Was he serious? I actually got to go somewhere?

I walked three miles from home to get to the skate party. I sat around awkwardly for about an hour until I decided to borrow some roller skates. I clumsily went around the rink twice until I felt embarrassed and gave up. A girl walked up to me as I sat in the corner, thinking I wasn't actually going to have fun.

The girl smiled, "Do you know how to dance?"

I stuttered, "A little. I practice sometimes, but I could learn better if you don't mind teaching me."

I learned how girls dance and practiced with them on the carpeted floor until I made friends that wanted to dance with me on the skate floor. I learned how much fun it could be to move your body to music, or at least the simple version of how to twerk. It was freeing. The enjoyment what other people felt skating, I had dancing. If a boy got behind me, I would move, as I wasn't ready for that just yet. I was learning how to lure boys without the desire to lure them. I was just learning how to dance, missing the sexual appeal entirely. The girls just wanted me to dance. Somehow I was surrounded by a mass of people. They began to shout out what I should do to dance better.

A voice shouted, "Rub your belly with one hand and your head with the other." *Was this a version of the macarena?*

Another voice shouted, "She looks like a duck! Quack ducky! Quack!"

I wasn't very good at dancing yet. I was surrounded by people mocking me, but that didn't stop me from trying harder. I just hadn't practiced enough. The moves weren't smooth enough. I needed a mirror to show me how to perfect my moves to truly be something to look at.

While I was gone, security cameras were set up in the room I shared with Orion. The commander only wanted to ensure I was keeping a watchful eye on my little brother, right?

What's the harm if you only have a fatherly intention?

I only found out the following year. Business continued as usual. The only suspicion I had was a constant paranoia of the feeling that I was being watched. One time I saw a glimpse of our room plastered on the big screen TV in the living room, an image of my body hunched over as I learned how to twerk better. Rob turned it off as soon as I caught a glimpse. I didn't say anything. I tried being more careful by covering everything that might be a camera with a blanket to keep him from spying on me anymore. The blankets were often removed at some point each day.

It was a week before fifth grade began, at the end of summer. Rob came home while Orion and I were having lunch, our daily meal of stovetop ramen.

Rob walked in and asked, "What are you doing, little girl?"

I stared blankly as I retorted, "I'm making lunch."

He smiled his sly, sideways grin, "So you don't have time for games?"

"Games," I said, "We don't play any games."

Rob went to the freezer and picked up a piece of ice from the tray.

He held it at the nape of my neck and smiled, "Sure, I think you like playing games."

He dropped the ice in the back of my underwear, so I picked it out and placed it inside his shirt pocket. Orion got up and put a piece of ice inside the top of Rob's button-up shirt. It slid all the way down to his belly, leaving a snail-like trail.

Rob took off his shirt after declaring it ruined for the rest of the day, and grabbed another ice cube from the freezer. He slid the cube in the front of Orion's underwear. Orion yipped and giggled until he got it out and placed it in the trash, and sat back down to continue eating.

I grabbed a new ice cube and pushed it into the back of Rob's pants, pulling at his belt so it would go down and wouldn't easily be removed. Rob undid his belt, grabbed the ice cube, and walked towards me with his pants sneaking down slowly.

I tried to run, but instead stumbled into the living room, tripping over one of Rob's storage boxes that littered the floor. Rob held out his hand to seem like he would help me up after I fell. I allowed the game to continue by taking his hand and being escorted up

Rob pushed me against the wall and slid my panties to the side, pushing the ice inside of the hole that the worm had dug. I slid down the floor against the wall and burst into tears and laughter. Rob's bulbous body pressed against mine as his finger held the ice deep within my hole.

I squealed, laughing, "Stop! stop!"

His smile was bigger than I had ever seen, lacking the asymmetry it had every time I had seen him smile.

He whispered, his face pressed to my ear, "If you want me to stop, then why are you laughing, little slave? You must enjoy it."

I gasped nervously, trying not to laugh, "I don't know. I just want it to stop. Please. Stop." He wiggled the ice inside deeper and only released his grip when it melted. He licked his finger and stood up. He slithered out the front door and took off in his car.

I went into my closet and wailed out sobs of regret. I took all the stolen items and arranged them on the floor as I gasped for the tears to stop. I began to hide the items inside of my stuffed animals, at the top of the closet, and into the storage door in the closet's ceiling. I was getting ready to steal faster than before. I wanted to take everything I could. I didn't care if I was caught now. I wanted to hurt him the only way I could. I wanted the growing lost feeling inside of my bones, a hollow sensation deep within, to cease. It was becoming all that I could feel.

I began to steal the dildos lined against Rob's bed frame in messy rows. There were too many to count, ideal for thievery. There were already some that had fallen from the headboard under the bed. I took everything I found in excess. Anything I could get my hands on that I knew might be missed, with self-blame remaining possible. I wasn't just stealing out of secretive bins anymore. I stole from wallets, makeup bags, and purses too. I would have gotten away with it, except I didn't know about the cameras.

Rob approached me, months later, after school and growled, "Little girl, what did you do to my magnums?"

"...What I don't," I muttered, confused.

He yelled, "The condoms, the big black box with the rubbers in it. Where did you put them?"

I backed away, stuttering, "I didn't take...."

He shouted, "I don't care if you took them for your boyfriend. His tiny prick is too small, I bet, not like mine. These take a huge cock to fill them. I bet you'd like that, wouldn't you? I haven't given it to you yet, but I will. I'm just biding my time. I bet you couldn't get enough of the feel of a big fat dick in your tight little slot."

Strangely, I had never seen any condoms.

I whimpered, "I don't know what that is."

He smiled, "I need them because sex feels good. So good. I'm trying to have loads of it with your mom. Do you know what that's like? Do you need me to show you? Sex feels SO good. I'm going to give it to your mother tonight and maybe you afterwards if you're lucky."

I shook my head, "No. I don't want that. No."

I scrambled off to my room and hid in the closet.

I had never thought about it, but if sex felt good, I needed to try it before it became some decree of needing it done by him. I felt the need to feel it before I lost the chance to never enjoy it again. I became disturbed with worry that one of the spider's check-ins might involve rape. He had already gotten everything else despite my every action of going against his will. How could I take it away from him?

The next day, I was caught on camera stuffing cigarettes inside one of my stuffed animals. After school, Rob called me into the kitchen and asked me to sit down.

He sat beside me and gruffed, "So I went through your room today. You want to tell me what I might have found?"

I lied, knowing the answers he wanted, "Umm... Clothes, shoes, probably some trash, stuffed animals."

He cheered, "Stuffed animals. Ah, let's talk about that. What were in the animals?"

I pretended to think, "Stuffing. So like cotton or whatever that fluff is."

He slammed his hands on the table and grimaced. I smiled after I reflexively jumped.

This interrogation wasn't going as timely as he had imagined. Was I just supposed to confess and plead for forgiveness? I'm <u>NOT</u> sorry.

He sighed, "So what about the lipstick? The cigarettes? I don't remember you smoking. I should have bought you a whole carton and watched you smoke them all up until you're vomiting and sick."

"I don't smoke," I replied, "Why don't you go smoke a whole carton and Lysol the bathroom until it runs out like you always do."

He looked at me, musing, "OK, fine. Forget it. I smoke. That's why they're my cigarettes. It doesn't matter what I do in the bathroom or what I do with my body, for that matter. Let's talk about something else. Let's debate why you stole dildos from your mother. Did you use them? What did you think they were?"

I huffed, "I didn't use them. I thought they were sculptures. They're so uh... interesting looking, right?"

The interrogation went on for three hours. For the last hour, my only response was, "I don't know," regardless of the question. I had stopped listening.

What ended the entire thing was Rob's frustration. He grabbed a handful of dish soap from the sink behind us and stuck his hand in my mouth until I gagged so many times I vomited on his hand.

He stomped out the door without even washing his hands. The taste of soap ravaged my tongue and throat, although terrible, bitter-sweet. At that moment, the repugnance I felt for him mirrored back at me in his tone, time, action, and the repulsed look in his eyes. I wasted hours of his time on a pointless interrogation and didn't break as he hoped.

There was a sense of beauty within it. He despised me too much to find me beautiful anymore. The spider came out of hiding his true form just a little as the days went on.

I lived to make monsters show themselves. To make them unable to wear the mask they love so well.

Please don't try this at home.

Or do.

Just be careful.

8. The Grey

In all the recent chaos that life threw at me, I never thought to check for monsters. They had come to me before, the shadows and demons, but I had stopped noticing them with such evil in the house belonging to a human. There was no bed to check under. The closet was my underworld. I had nothing that could belong to the shadows. My body and mind were under constant surveillance of the spider, so maybe the dark shadows didn't like competition.

Every day I watched Rob spin my Mom further into his distorted web. I was tortured with the effects of neglect, sexual abuse, and why either had occurred. He was the only evil that could torture me. Or was, until I fell prey to a shapeshifter. It wasn't the first time I had encountered it. It had taken over Tommy's body. This creature followed me even in my darkest days, only invisibly in the shadows. I named the demon Grey because its coloring was the only thing that never changed. The one constant was Grey was always gray, even if it appeared as a cat, dog, wolf, human, or some combination of those things. Grey just chose when he wanted to make an appearance when a good time to find a body might be to appear normal until you could look into his eyes and know that was no ordinary animal. Coming on his own without a recent corpse, the form he became was never the same, indistinguishable between man, wolf, and cat. He only appeared most often as a cat because they have always been my favorite animal that I admired as guardians from the dark world. It was a ploy to turn my love into fear and disdain. A way to never accept a cat to protect me ever again. It never worked.

The first occasion I met Grey at this house was about a

month after I was allowed to feed the stray cats outside. Mom bought me a giant bag of *Friskies* so I could feed as many strays as often as I liked. I provided for all the neighboring cats, including a litter of kittens that were kindled nearby. My favorite part of every day was feeding them. They were too feral to pet, but watching them eat was enough joy for me.

I was filling up the food bowls for the cats when the solitary Grey appeared from nowhere and came slithering slowly toward the clutter of cats. It didn't move like the others. I had never seen Grey move up until this point. I only ever heard the cries he made out of a corpse. He never got too close to me until now. Grey's eyes were unlike any other feline because he wasn't really ever a cat. They were just as gray as his fur but reflected a glow of yellow. Even in the blinding sun, the closer he crawled, the more yellow his eyes appeared. It was like an optical illusion; yellow meets gray, into yellow on repeat. Grey's eyes remained locked within mine for the entirety of his appearance. The demon kept moving closer, but I never saw his legs move. The ground moved underneath him. Instead, the Earth moved for him to give him the ability to walk. As he reached the kittens, their bodies moved like a parted sea, as if trained to move away if they ever crossed paths. I turned to rush into the house as fear-based adrenaline flooded my veins. I stopped in my tracks, thinking of saving the kittens. But how? I grabbed a metal beam outside the house and rushed off the porch, waving my weapon like a maniac at Grey. I cared nothing for what he might do to me. I was terrified, yet I had to protect the innocent lives I tried to keep alive.

The gray creature took a step back, this time by moving its legs. I rammed the beam into the single oak tree in the yard and yelled, "Get out! Get away from them! I don't know what you are, but you're not like them! I see you. Go away and never come back!" The demon only went as far as the driveway. Trying anymore seemed a fruitless endeavor. I was only scaring the kindle of cats. As the days went by, fewer kittens appeared. No strays came to eat after a while. I was only left with a bag of food and Grey.

    I left a single bowl of cat food out in the yard for when, or if, they decided to come back. Grey never ate. It only came to stare. I stopped putting food out when I found two big stray dogs devouring the food left in the bowl one morning on my way to school. I have feared large stray dogs since I was chased in first grade.

    Even the dogs didn't scare Grey away. They didn't seem able to see him.

    He only disappeared about a month later after I adopted an old stray cat named Jade, that allowed me to pet him. He had gray peppered fur with black stripes and the greenest jade eyes. I stared into his vibrant eyes while he devoured an entire bowl of food. He let me pet him while he ate, never growling, and even stopped to receive additional pets, despite being close to starvation. Jade would come to visit twice a day to be fed and receive cuddles.

    A few weeks after finding Jade, Rob arrived home with a six-month-old kitten that had been following him around his workplace. It was a beautiful long-haired Seal-point Siamese with dark cement gray markings and dusty white fur. His eyes were the most stunning shade of aquamarine.

    As a kitten, he loved to play and chase anything he found around the house. Except for a tarantula.

    A tarantula was hiding in the clutter of boxes encompassing the living room and chased up onto Rob's office chair. I stood there for a solid thirty minutes, yelling at the cat to help me, but he was nowhere to be found. I was fine with leaving the spider alone. I just didn't want it to chase or to touch me. I've never liked spiders. Nothing came to the rescue, so after waiting half an hour, I jumped down and ran into my room. Sapphire, the kitten, was lounging on Rob's bed lazily. We were frenemies after that.

    As he got older, he became feral with lust. The lust turned to my leg so he would leave Rob's bed to sneak into my room and hump my leg incessantly. I slept on the floor, so there was no escape. I tried pushing him off and kicking him, but he'd only come back with a vengeance as his eyes turned red. Something had infected him, and he had become a monster. He was not the Grey, but something else.

When I complained to Mom about it, she told Rob, who said, "Just let him finish. Stop complaining about a little kitten hunching your leg. Let him do his business, and he'll move along." The humping went on for hours as I tried to go to sleep. I tried to cocoon myself into my sheet so I wouldn't feel his wet spikes trying to penetrate my leg. I no longer liked this cat at all. He was pretty, but there was some sort of devil within him. I've always been popular with monsters.

It finally stopped when Jade walked a tiny tabby kitten home with him on one of his daily visits. Mom fell in love with her instantly and allowed her kitten and Jade inside. Jade often spent his time outside wandering around, as he was a wild cat after all.

Sapphire began to try to woo Mom's kitten with gifts of mice that inhabited the house, letting her eat first and bathing her constantly. When she went into heat, he had his chance to relieve all of the tensions that had been stored. Gremlin, the new mother, gave birth to their kittens in Mom's closet. Mom and I watched the birth from the closet door and noticed she only opened the placenta sacs that resembled her. Most of the kittens were black somehow, and none looked like Sapphire. They didn't even have his eyes. Mom gently opened the rest of the sacs with her hands so they would survive. Seven kittens were born, but the runt came out excessively weak and died the following day. It was one of the kittens that looked like her. She abandoned it with the black kittens in the closet and moved her twins to the other side of Mom's room underneath the headboard. Mom constantly had to help the other kittens get to Gremlin to ensure their survival. I named all of them basic names as they would be rehomed as soon as they were able. Sapphire had no interest in his possible children. He must not have been certain if he was the daddy. Jade had no interest in mating with her, obviously treating her as his child and making a disgusted face when Gremlin would try to seduce him.

Mom was always cooing at the kittens instead of seeking orders from Rob. Anytime Gremlin made a nest with her kittens on the bed, he'd throw them off, yelling about her making a mess with her rat babies.

One day he grew weary of yelling and throwing them all against the wall, so he grabbed Gremlin by the nape of her neck, took her to the bathroom, turned the water on, and shut the plexiglass shower door to lock her in. She was yowling, practically screaming for help, for a full ten minutes. The water was steaming hot. He stood at the bathroom door to ensure no one would rescue her until Mom pleaded enough to be allowed entry, muttering, "I guess that's long enough."

Mom cried, "Gremmie, I'm coming for you, baby."

Mom opened the shower door, turned off the water, and called out for Gremlin, whose voice had turned to a horse screeching and was nowhere to be found. Mom was in tears searching for her until finding her inside the shower wall, in front of the tub. How she got in there was a mystery, but Mom broke the end of the drywall, creating a big enough hole to grab her by her arms and pull her out. Gremlin was drenched, wet, and terrified.

Rob laughed, "Since she didn't stay the full time, I guess we'll have to do it again."

Mom scowled, "That's about enough. More than enough. What the hell is wrong with you?"

He explained, "That's what the bitch gets messing up my bed. It's disgusting.

Mom huffed back, "Then let me clean it up. If it's your bed, I guess I'll sleep somewhere else instead. I'll change your sheets twenty times if I have to. Leave my cat alone. Worry about yours instead."

Rob sighed, "I didn't mean it like that."

Mom murmured some more words that led to Rob driving off somewhere in his car without returning for a few hours until much later that night.

Gremlin was never the same after this event. She refused to feed her kittens as if they didn't belong to her. If they got too close, she would hiss. She no longer desired affection, becoming more of a street cat, wanting nothing of her indoor life. She never purred. She only returned home for food and grew skittish to attention until she was only seen a couple times a week. Sapphire spent more time with the kittens, taking over Gremlin's job in her absence, except he couldn't provide the needed nourishment of breast milk that Gremlin carried. Mom bought wet food for them and gave them up as outside cats so Rob wouldn't complain anymore. Sapphire also cared for them outside, although he preferred to be an indoor cat. The kittens stayed in the yard, and I kept them fed as best as possible.

9. Knowledge and Depression

During sixth grade, I was overcome with a bout of depression after taking a course on sexual education. Despite wanting to lose my virginity so Rob couldn't take it, I knew very little about things of that nature. I didn't menstruate until the end of the year, so all I knew about my vagina was that I peed with it. I wasn't entirely sure what sex was, even though I had caught glances of the act several times.

My curiosity never peaked to find out how it was done. Sex-ed was a vital lesson educating me about my body, teaching me there had always been another hole. I learned about all the parts, names, and diseases that could occur from not using protection during intercourse. Our lesson plan was a dual course on drug and alcohol training. I didn't know what drugs were, even if that made me seem naive. It was the first time I had ever heard about their existence. It made me curious to try some of them out, to feel better and less like me. It seemed like a dream.

I had smelled skunk-scented cigarettes before, but I didn't think it was marijuana. Who was supposed to teach you everything in this class, if not the class itself? Sixth grade was the perfect age to learn.

I spent the next few weeks of school with my head on my desk, arms cradling my face, and covering my desk in tears. The lessons went on as usual. Only a couple of kids near me would ask me what was wrong. My response was a hollow, "Don't worry about it."

It wasn't until a teacher I didn't know but had always noticed because of her sphynx-like beauty, requested my presence in the hall.

I was crying through another geography lesson when the

teacher asked, "Storm, why don't you go in the hall?"

It didn't seem unusual for her to kick me out of her class. I distracted her from teaching and the other kids from paying full attention to her lesson. I wiped my tears from the table with my arm and slouched out the door. I expected to lean against the wall outside and slide myself down to flow into cradling myself, but as I stepped out, I was in the presence of Missus. Fawn.

Missus Fawn had an exotic kind of beauty. Soft, worn bleached leather was the composition of her skin. Speckled silver and gray hair fell into her face, framing her perfectly lined cat eyes. She was the kind of woman that appeared in designer perfume ads.

I had never been this close to her before. I had only seen her from afar while walking to one of my other classes, admiring her smile as she taught in her small classroom with the door open. Studying her beauty took my solace to a halt. Her pale outlined lips smiled softly. Her voice was as beautiful as her appearance.

She spoke confidently, "Hello, Stormy. I just wanted to check in to see if there's anything at all I can do to help you. A pretty girl like you should never have to cry."

Tears filled my eyes as I was embarrassed the beautiful sphynx had noticed me because of my endless tears.

She hushed like the sun on a chill-filled morning, "Shh... It's alright. It's okay to cry. It takes the pain away. I cry sometimes. My husband... Well, my husband is overseas, in the military. He's on his fifth tour.. so I get it. I miss him so much sometimes that I cry because I feel alone. Is it like that? Or is something more... more serious wrong? Did something happen? We could talk about it if you want. My classroom is empty right now. We could go in there for however long you like. But if you would prefer not to talk to me...."

I shook my head and sniffed my nose, leaking from excessive tears.

She smiled sombrely, "That's okay too. I have some friends I can refer you to and set up an appointment with their counseling group. It could really help you. It's a non-profit, so it won't cost a thing. I'll set a date and call your parents to see if they can take you."

She assured me, "I won't tell your parents why I'm giving you a referral, just that it could be beneficial if you go. Would that be all right? All I want to do is help give you the resources you deserve. I want to see your beautiful smile again. I've seen you in the hallways before. You never needed my class. Well, I teach kids that need a little extra help from time to time. From what I hear, you're brilliant. You're one of the top students in your class."

I smiled, whispering, "I'd like that. Thank you, Mrs. Fawn."

She smiled back graciously, her eyes sparkling with tears as she asked, "Can I give you a hug?"

I wrapped my arms around her and felt the love resonate within her, the feeling Mom used to have. Hugging her made me feel like I was three years old again. I didn't want to let her go. I returned to the room I had left, smiling as I resumed the lesson with the rest of the class.

One person can make a difference.

When I arrived home from school, Mom and Rob sat in the living room, reviewing some papers. I wasn't too concerned until I saw the front cover of one of my notebooks. These books contained everything I ever wrote. I was about to be in a lot of trouble. I wrote my ugliest thoughts down on the back pages of journals. My deepest secrets, things no one should ever know. I scribbled in the back of all the journals so they'd never be found. I wrote hate speech galore, tucked away, hidden in those pages. I never wanted to not exist more than I did at this moment. I went to my room and lay face down in my bed of blankets on the floor. I was impatiently torpid and waiting on whatever was going to be said after those pages had been read. After all my secrets had been spilled, I wanted to get it over with but rushing it was pointless. I chose to lie lifeless and pretend to suffocate in bed. If I died right now, it would be a relief from the feeling I endured as they read all the thoughts in my head... Hours passed until it was dark outside when Mom entered my room.

Orion happily sat watching something on the box-set television, humming to himself.

Mom whispered, "Hey, Babygirl, are you awake? We need to talk."

I sighed heavily, "I'm awake," and followed her to her dark blue Saturn.

She wanted to talk in the car where no one else could hear, explaining nervously, "I wish we could talk about this over ice cream or something. I'd take you somewhere... I don't know what's open at this hour, and it's not so private talking there. Let's see... Um... So I read through your journals. You really don't like Rob, do you? You don't like his age difference, his personality, or his appearance. You seem to really dislike him. There was a lot of that. Mmm... You also wrote a few things about me. It was all really dark. Strangely pretty. But dark, cruel even. You have a lot of strong feelings, don't you? Did you mean what you wrote?"

I wasn't sure how to respond. *Of course, I meant what I wrote. It was all the thoughts I kept repressed in my head. All my abhorrence, misdeeds, and things that had been done to me were written on those pages. I wiggled in my seat uncomfortably, uncertain of how to get out of this mess. I promised to always be Mom's star because I didn't think she had one. I tried to be kind. I sighed, knowing I couldn't possibly tell her she was only a shell of herself, and I couldn't see the light within her any longer. She was too far spun in her spider's web, and that spider was an absolute monster, a monster without an end.*

Boarding school had already been threatened upon me, a prison of young girls. That's not what scared me. It's what the next step afterward would be. What punishment would occur if I told nothing but the truth? I bet I'd be homeless. Rob was her master, her everything. *If she knew what he wanted to do to me, I could be beaten with the whip Rob occasionally beat Orion with when he didn't do what he wanted. He never left marks, but it was a bullwhip, so I can't imagine the fear and pain involved. He never touched him as he did me, so he received the same sick punishment, just done a different way. I could be tossed outside like a stray animal. I could be tied up in a trunk and left to die somewhere. I could simply disappear without a trace, but before disappearing, I bet Rob would show me what it was like to be raped. I can't imagine that feeling remotely pleasant. I'd be puking or laughing the entire time, possibly even both. Would Mom protect me if she thought I was her competition? Would she even notice? He could just tell her he sent me to boarding school. The truth wouldn't do me any favors.*

After rummaging through the trainwreck of my mind, I lied, "I was just sad and angry. I just never see you anymore. I don't feel loved. Things aren't like the way they used to be."
Every lie has some fragment of truth embedded within it.

I couldn't dare break her heart. I couldn't look into her sapphire eyes and tell her everything she did wrong. Informing her of how she failed, made me feel like absolute nothing, or that I couldn't possibly be her daughter anymore because she didn't treat me like one. In saying the words, I felt betrayed by myself, but I knew I was protecting her. She was still my angel, even if nothing of her angelic nature was left.

She hummed under her breath, pondering her next question. *Or to leave a silence where I might be expected to talk if she couldn't think of the next thing to say. It's a part of social etiquette. The period in which I was locked in a room may have been the designated age for this particular social nicety. Silent moments are my natural state. Quiet can come as a relief from all of the noise that revolves around the world. Awkward pauses only up my anxiety, but no thoughts occur, at least not any that I care to share out loud. I often become even more silent, if at all possible.*

After a forceful breath, Mom asked, "So what about this Murray fellow? Who is that? Did that really happen?"

I sighed, "You know, Murray. Your friend. The guy you

hugged when we pulled up to see Iris when you left me for a week before we moved to Georgia."

Her mouth formed a silent 'O'.

Afterward, she squeaked, "You sure? Him? I knew him. He wasn't really my friend. He used to come to Waffle House at night, and we'd talk for hours while I worked. He was one of my best customers."

I dryly replied, "Yeah... that's the guy. He had a daughter my age. We spent the night at his house together."

She looked down at the floorboard and whispered, "I'm sorry."

I shrugged, "It's fine. It happened."

WHY was she asking me these things?? She had already read everything she asked in great detail. I wasn't writing horror fiction. I was writing all the secrets inside my head.

Next question... I was getting tired of this line of questioning. I just wanted to know my punishment. To go back to bed, I already knew... I get to go nowhere. I talk to no one. I no longer get to hold a pen. I might have my head shaved again and have to dig a tunnel that goes from one side of the house to the other. And once I finish, fill it all in with the dirt taken out. Maybe I'll dig into Mexico or China and really spice things up. I might even get my door back and the siren put back on it.

Come on, hurry up. Carry on, but hurry up.

I had more patience for Mom even if I wasn't patient in my head. I wanted to leave the car with how this entire conversation dragged out. What's the point? I would've already talked about it if I wanted to.

Mom really spoke to me. Never for this long.

Maybe I should try to enjoy it despite the line of questioning. Was something said about ice cream? I could really go for some peppermint-chip. I never said any of this, though. I just sat there in the dark of the car beside her. Has she always been this pale? Her skin looked melted from her bones. Was I that pale? I started staring at my hand. I couldn't be so sure sitting there in the dark.

Mom stuttered, unable to form words. She continued,

"Okay... So, Rob... you wrote that Rob did the same thing to you. Just with ice."

A dramatic sigh mouth through my lips. My face fell in my hands reflexively as I shook my head. Somehow this was mistaken for no, if only because she wanted it to be.

She smiled gleefully, "Great. It didn't happen. Go in and sit on your dad's lap and tell him you're sorry, that you know he would never, ever do that to you. Call him Dad. And it will all be over. He'll forgive you. We just want this whole matter cleared away and swept under the rug. You got confused from when it happened before. It's OK. Just go sit on his lap and tell him that."

I sputtered, removing my head from my hands, "But it **did** happen."

She smiled sideways, just as Rob did, "You got confused, capiche? You know what you must do to make this all go away."

She was trying to brainwash me!

Hello, lady spider, wearing a mom suit. You really had me going there, just for a minute. I thought we were having a slow-moving mother-daughter talk. I see you now. Fine. It's all just... peachy.... Great.

As I stepped out of the car, I looked to the sky, looking for my star. I prayed for my fallen star to give me the courage to power through this catastrophe, but there were no stars in the sky. All of the stars were gone. The sky was black. I had to be strong on my own.

I walked through the front door where the Huntsman Spider sat in his desk chair he used as a throne, his lap ready to be sat on.

The talk was just a show. Nobody cares. I was too old to sit in anyone's lap, but I did as the lady spider instructed and took my seat.

I stammered out my lines, "I'm sorry, Rob. I know you would... never do that to me... with what I wrote. I'm sorry I-I... got confused."

I did all that was instructed except call him Dad. Nobody but my deadbeat father could carry that title. I forced a smile.

Rob whispered in my ear so nobody else could hear, "I

forgive you, my pretty little slave girl. You're such a good girl."

I stood up slowly to keep the scene intact. Mom was watching. The show was over. Rob mistook my devotion to Mom as subservience to him. In his mind, he had finally won. I hated it when he called me a good girl. It was the furthest thing I wanted to be for him.

An hour later, I came out of my room because I had not eaten dinner.

While trying to cross through Mom's room, I saw Rob standing on his knees in their bed.

Mom was crouched down, kneeling, pleading, "No, Master, no! Please! No, it hurts so bad. Stop, please, master."

Rob was attempting to sodomize her. Apparently, she wasn't as willing as she usually was for other acts of sex or degradement. He needed a hole that was seldom used to celebrate his victory. I walked backward to get to my room and tried to not think about Mom getting anal raped by her owner.

I went to therapy for the first time a few days later. Mom handed my therapist the notebooks so they had a baseline to go off of.

The notebooks were returned to me the same day, with the counselor saying, "I'd rather hear it from you than invade your privacy with whatever you wrote in these books. These are sacred. Write as much as you can whenever you can. Get it all out. It's healthy to do."

I threw my spirals in the trash before leaving. If there was no privacy, there was no point. I returned to therapy twice a week but didn't say much. I spoke about why I had been crying, but for the most part, I drew, talked about my day at school, and ate muffins in their break room. I changed counselors three times until one stuck with me, but no breakthroughs occurred. My therapy sessions dropped once every two weeks, stating I was in recovery. There was no recovery; I just didn't speak. Not about anything soul-splitting, at least. Eventually, I stopped going. There was no point since I didn't want to talk. I didn't see the reason to go since I made everything up.

The best thing about the summer after the sixth grade was the weekly outings with Mrs. Fawn. She would pick me up from home with another girl named Rose, who lived a few streets over. We went on trips to the library to pick out different books, and afterward, we'd get a bite to eat at the tea garden. She paid no matter what we ordered, although it was often a cup of iced tea out of a fancy wine glass. The tea selection consisted of flavorings like sweet peaches, tart raspberries, or juicy blackberries to choose from, served both hot and cold. It felt so fancy and free. Like I was worth going to a place such as this. I left all of my problems at home.

Our outings were all about moral support and reminding us that we matter, to bring light into our otherwise dark world. I never asked Rose why she had been chosen, but she never asked me either. It didn't matter. We just enjoyed the company of the kind teacher that never taught us in school. Rose was one of the few that surpassed me in the reading competition that went on at school. I read a lot, but not half as much as her.

Mrs. Fawn taught us that good people still care even when it feels like no one ever could. She never asked any questions. She just smiled and drove. It was the first time I didn't hate summer. I had her to thank for that.

10. Life of the Party

My hair had grown so much that it was down to the end of my back. I had been taking hair vitamins since my head had been shaved in the summer of third grade. Boys finally began to think I was pretty again.

I was allowed to go to the lock-in overnight skate event once more.

Orion was taken to see a play in Dallas of his favorite TV show, *Bear in the Big Blue House on Ice*.

My subservience gave us both more privileges. It almost made me wish I had rebelled a little less.

I walked to the skating rink, determined to find a boyfriend that night. I didn't meet a keeper, but I danced until I gained the interest of many eyes. I was felt up by three different guys by the time the party was over. I kissed five people. I never got any of their names. I didn't care when I felt like the life of the party. This is what freedom was like.

I started 7th grade at the school I chose called *Barwise Junior High*. It was a performing arts school, which seemed much more interesting than the other options. There was a school where uniforms were required, where everything was gray and white. The other school's highlight was math. Neither of those seemed very appealing.

Little did I know, Barwise was an undercover school for misfits. Gangs ran rampant, and if you weren't part of some clique, you were a victim. It was a juvenile detention center labeled as a school, except there were no guards.

My locker was vandalized at least twice a week. How the

vandals knew the combination when I so frequently forgot was impressive.

At lunch, students took turns being my personal bully. I never ate as I was on a strict air diet at school and home. I didn't get my food taken or lunch money stolen as I didn't have either.

Instead, I was berated with insults. *At least I was popular.* Every day someone didn't eat just to talk down to me as I stared at the table, mute, with tears in my eyes.

After lunch, random kids would push and trip me, but I only fell once. *At least I had a good balance.*

A couple months after school started, Mom and Rob took Orion and me to a carnival in town. I couldn't remember a single time I had ever been to a fair. It would've been fascinating if I had been younger. It was entertaining but not as impressive as Orion thought it was.

Orion was in bliss-filled heaven, staring at all the brightly colored lights and spinning rides. His face was a portrait of enchantment.

The rides were fun, but something, or rather someone, caught my attention more.

He required no bright lights aside from his hazel, light-filled eyes to mesmerize me. I wasn't sure how to get his attention or how to be allowed to exit 'family fun time' for this older stranger. He was seventeen, and I was only thirteen going on twenty-one in a hurry.

(To shed some light on my promiscuity, ten percent of women become hyper-sexual after abuse. It is a coping mechanism and an addiction. Most addicts have suffered some type of abuse in childhood, often before the age of eight.)

I was in luck. The handsome stranger's brother, Tony, a chubby, sweet geek in my AP English class, happily came over upon seeing me.

He met my family and courteously requested, "I'd love it if you could go on some rides with us. I understand if you're having family time, but it would be amazing if we could hang out. Could you?"

I smiled gleefully at Mom, "May I?"

Mom leaned against Rob, playfully humming, "Oh, I don't know. What do you think, my love?"

He nodded, "Go ahead. Just meet us back here in two hours."

I cheered, "Thank you! Thank you, guys, so much!"

They must have felt so relieved I was excited to hang out with Tony. He appeared entirely harmless.

The situation was a bit twisted. My classmate thought I was excited to spend time with him when I had only found an opportunity to spend time with his older brother, who was a complete stranger.

The three of us rode a few rides together until I whispered to the handsome stranger, Drew, "These rides are fun, but if only I could ride you." I thought about it since I first saw him but felt shy until I couldn't contain the thought any longer. Keeping the thought secret felt like burning molten lava inside my pelvic floor.

His smile was just as stunning as his eyes.

He chuckled as he blew his hair from his eyes and responded casually, "Just tell me when and where."

I giggled, holding back my full excitement, as butterflies fluttered inside my stomach and chest. It was like dropping to the bottom of a high rollercoaster, almost nauseating if not entirely pleasant.

I brushed against Drew's arm and took a deep breath to remain calm and sensuous as I whispered, "Let's look around. Show me where that ride is."

He excused himself away from me to talk to Tony. He gave him a few dollars to spend while he was gone.

Tony protested for a moment, "Mom told us to stick together. You're supposed to be watching me. We can all have fun together. Let's ride some more rides and get some food. Storm was my friend first. If anything, I should ask *you* to let me be alone with *her*. She doesn't know you. You're just my older brother. You're too old to be with her anyways. It's not fair."

Drew replied, "She's about to get to know me *really* well. I'll be back in an hour. Just get some food and ride a ride or two, and I'll be back soon. Meet me here so mom won't find out. I'll make it up to you, okay? I promise."

Tony looked down and muttered, "Okay."

I held Drew's hand as we traveled through the carnival. He wasn't pushy about me keeping my word. He often stopped looking, so we could go on a ride or walk through a maze.

Going through a plexiglass maze, I hit my face hard on an invisible wall. Drew laughed as he bumped into me but stopped when he realized I hit my face.

He worried, "Are you OK, babe?"

He called me babe! My lust turned to love as he cared whether or not I had been hurt.

With my face throbbing in pain, I kissed him like his mouth was a ripe, delicate fruit that needed to be eaten with lips, tongue, and teeth combined.

He hummed, "I'll take that for a yes. Where did we decide on where to take this ride?"

I smiled, "Hmm... Let's see... Do you wanna ride the Ferris Wheel with me?"

He groaned dramatically but smiled as he said, "yes."

My body felt like flames dancing playfully in melting candle wax.

Once reaching the pinnacle of the Ferris wheel, I pulled my shirt up along with my bra to show him my naked breasts.

He smiled, "This really is the best ride of my life. I am so lucky I met you."

We kissed all the way to the bottom. His taste was sweet and musky, like saltwater from the ocean. Down at the bottom, my heart dropped at the sight of my mom.

I was informed that I was to never see that boy again. She did allow me to tell him goodbye and even kiss him afterwards. Mom and Rob, along with my brother, saw me flash Drew my bare chest. *How embarrassing.*

I spent the rest of the time at the carnival with my mom

on a ride called *'The Zipper'*. As it took off and flung us around, I screamed all the profanities my mind could conjure. At times, Mom was laughing so hard that she choked on the air that thrusted us around. At the end of the ride, she exclaimed, "Oh my God, Storm. I didn't know you knew all of those words. I didn't even know half of those phrases." I smiled, "Do you wanna do it again?"

After spending time with Drew, I needed something to release the euphoria flooding my brain.

I spent three days wondering how to get in touch with Drew. Finally, I had a brilliant idea.

I asked Tony during AP English if he would mind giving a letter to his brother from me. He agreed reluctantly.

The next day I wrote a letter confessing my undying love, asking Drew if he might ever feel the same way. It was a bit dramatic, but I felt like a prisoner of his love, and I wanted no escape.

He was out of town with his Dad for the week, but I finally received a note back when he returned home.

I had to find a way to get to him.

I bribed a girl at school to be my friend and take me to see Drew. Mom had bought me gothic jewelry for my birthday last month, so I gave it to her, hoping she would follow through with my plan. I gave her my most valuable possession, a leather strapped watch with a large clock face depicting a fairy inside. It was beautiful but seeing Drew meant more to me than anything.

When she met Rob at our house after school, she claimed we had to work on a school project. All the supplies were at her house, so we needed to go over there to complete it. He agreed since it was for school.

I was supposed to be grounded after the carnival. I couldn't go anywhere, and I had to watch a horror movie every night to show me how dangerous strangers can be, but getting a good grade released me.

Her mom took us back to their house. Afterwards, I walked a couple streets down and met Drew at a stop sign where his road ended.

Drew's mom had also spied on us at the carnival, so he was forbidden from seeing me because it was apparent I was much younger than him. Our age gap could get him in a lot of trouble. It seemed unfair, but she was just trying to look out for him. Our love was forbidden by all, but it didn't matter to either of us.

It may have been even more exhilarating because of that fact. He was a rebel too.

I lost my virginity a few blocks from his house, under a bypass bridge just off the main highway.

It was the exit his mom took to get home from work. The possibility of someone seeing us felt a bit exciting. It reminded me of what Daisy had once said, *the bridge is where they do it*. It seemed legitimate to me.

It didn't matter the place. It only mattered that I fell in love with who I wanted. It was love at first sight. Any time I could sneak away with him, I did. I just had to tell somebody that I could talk to him ahead of time to avoid running into his mom. Sometimes he would call and sing to me. Life around me no longer mattered as long as I had him. He was my sanctuary.

This continued for three incredible months until Rob found all the letters Drew had written me.

It was a couple of weeks after he asked how the project was going, and I hesitated for far too long to actually have a school project. I tried to hide the letters because I couldn't bear throwing them away. After Rob found the things I had stolen before and the diary entries, nothing was safe anymore.

Mom picked me up from school, shouting from her car, "I can't believe you! I was so proud of you for still being a virgin. I'm so disappointed in you! Get in this car right now, young lady!"

I got in the car and had nothing to say.

She repeated, "Did you hear me? I'm so disappointed in you, Andromeda Storm."

I said, "OK, I heard you."

She scoffed, "When I was your age, if my mother, your

granny, had ever told me she was disappointed in me, it would have made me break down crying, begging her for forgiveness. You don't even look sad."

I replied, "I'm not you. I'm used to disappointing you. If I was sad every time I disappointed you, well... I had no idea you were ever proud of me,, so I would have to be sad all the time. I'm used to it. I disappoint you every day for my continued existence."

Mom slammed her hands down on the steering wheel as she growled and began to drive erratically to the police station.

She ordered, "Now you're going to tell them everything. Every little detail about that boy, you hear me?"

I said, "Okay."

We entered the police station and walked into an interrogation room filled with two chairs, a bean bag chair, and a two-way mirror that I'm sure Mom sat behind.

I confessed nothing, gave no vital information, and the little information I provided was false. I told the police Drew's name was Dre and made up a fake last name even though I knew the real one. I didn't even give any part of his real name that wasn't known.

I've never been the best liar, so an officer barked, "Do you know it's a federal offense to lie to an officer?"

I said yes without knowing the rules. Laws didn't matter to me. I wasn't breaking the law any more than anyone else was. *I think it's against the law to make a forced statement under duress.* It seemed like everyone was breaking the law.

This was the first time I had openly disobeyed Mom.

It was total bullshit. I gave myself to a person of my choosing and formed a bond that I would have willingly gone to jail for as long as it kept him safe. It wasn't his fault. It was mine. I was forced to be a grown-up, a chef, a mom, and her master's play toy.

If anyone should go to jail, it was Rob. If only I dared to confess his sins while I was taken to press charges against Drew. Too bad I didn't think about it until after the interrogation was over. Mom would've found out what it was like to be astoundingly disappointed with the smallest confession of her master Rob. It would've been worth it.

All the time I spent neglected and made to feel like a mistake, somehow I still had unconditional love for Mom, even when she granted amnesty to her pedophile and tried to imprison the man I love. I could be molested by two different grown men, and that's no reason to call the police. But for that same girl to fall in love and give her body freely was a horrendous crime. So what if he was a little bit older than me? He wasn't a fifty-year-old man. He wasn't sneaking away to molest me or force himself upon me. He was gentle, beautiful, and never did anything without me asking first. He let me be in charge, and I loved him for it.

Drew had not heard from me in a week since I was forced to make a false confession. I chose to not respond to his letters. I threw them away regrettably. He called my house, and I had to tell him we couldn't talk anymore. I confessed that my mom had taken me to the police station, but I ensured he was safe. He called once a month to say hello, tell me he missed me, and profess his undying love. But that was all that could be. I'd rather him be safe than be mine and forced to go to jail. Mom looked for him everywhere we went as if we could plan to meet up on unplanned visits to town. It was an irrational thought.

Trying to sneak off as much as I would have liked nothing more than just that wasn't safe.

It wasn't fair, but life rarely is.

Mom and Rob had a new girlfriend move in to take their relationship to the next level. She was a twenty-two-year-old from Guam named Gina. I liked her better than either of my caretakers because she was kind.

Mom said it was because she was closer to my age, but I didn't get along with much of anyone my age. I think it was her personality and how much she angered mom without ever trying.

Mom took me to a tattoo parlor with her to get Gina's name engraved on her ankle to make herself attached to her, but it didn't work. It was just a painful reminder that Gina lived in her home.

Sometimes Gina would watch scary movies with me. I was required to watch them to warn me of the dangers of men and the darkness of the world. *I obviously had no idea what that was like.* I had a scheduled scary movie hour, which I often extended for the entire day. My punishment had become entertainment.

My favorite movie out of all of them was *Strangeland*. Mom informed me it was also many serial killers' favorite movies, which made me a psychopath.

I replied, "Thanks for the compliment, Mom."

"If I weren't such a good person, I would slap you right now, and that will teach you," she growled.

She walked towards me in an attempt to frighten me.

I sat up straight and tilted my face to the side to make it easier for her.

She lifted her palm up but walked away at the last moment. As she walked away, Gina laughed, and I began to laugh along with her before continuing our movie.

Gina thought I was funny. She seemed to genuinely enjoy spending time with me and would even try to find the stray kittens with me and help me feed them. I liked her a lot. She was extremely easy to talk to and felt like a friend.

One time all of the household went to eat together at *On The Border*, and the adults ordered margaritas. Orion and I asked for *Shirly Temples*. When the drinks were brought to the table, the alcohol was given to Rob, Mom, and me. Surprisingly, Gina and Orion received the *Shirley Temples.*

Mom was furious at the server because this proved that I looked older than Gina. She let me take a drink while the server carded Gina before letting her have the drink I sipped from. I was never carded at any point. I even ordered a margarita of my own. It was funny that I looked like an adult sitting next to her. It was a beautiful moment for me because Mom was starting to see now that her glorious master was attracted to little girls.

Gina was his first choice because she had a baby face and had been shy when talking online. The truth was finally beginning to trickle down.

Mom had been spun within Rob's web for too many years. It lost its grasp when her Master tried to take his rage out on Orion.

Did he not notice her sitting on the bed as he pulled his bullwhip off its hook on the wall?

He tried to hide his monster form when she was around. But he had forgotten now.

Rob commanded, "Get in the corner now, you little faggot. I'll be coming for you."

Orion cowered down with his hands above his head as he began to head to the corner. It wasn't any new form of punishment, nor any new insults. It was his preferred way to deal with my brother. I had only ever been whipped in the corner once before. Luckily Orion didn't get in trouble very often. It only happened when the spider was in the mood to cause harm. Orion rarely did anything at all wrong. I did enough to keep negative attention away from Orion and onto myself.

On this occasion, Orion wanted to sing Mom a song from one of the *Disney* CDs in her CD case.

He was going to take it to our room, but Mom insisted, "You can play it here on my stereo, sweetie. It's fine."

He reluctantly placed it in her stereo to play. Since he was in their room, inside their walls of metal shelving where no one was to go, he would be beaten for trespassing.

Mom shouted, "Don't you dare touch him."

Mom had only once yelled at Rob. That was the one positive thing about their relationship.

She was his puppet, his lady spider. You can't yell at a

puppet, and a puppet can certainly not yell back at you.

Rob stammered, "He was in our room, the dirty little bastard."

"I told him he could. He had my permission. He did exactly what he was told. And don't yell at my children that way. What's your malfunction?"

He huffed, "But he knows better and he is a bastard."

Mom hissed, "Fine. Then I need permission to leave. I'm done with you."

Rob dropped his whip and walked towards Mom. I walked Orion over to our room, and put clothes on him. I walked him to the backyard so we wouldn't hear anything more.

Yelling could occasionally be heard from the house in the backyard, but the words were inaudible. We stayed outside for an hour until it seemed safe enough to go back inside.

Mom arranged for the three of us to move into a two-bedroom apartment in town. She changed jobs to be a store manager to make more money. Everything was set for the big move. She even made a pet deposit so we could get a cat.

It was the weekend before our date to move in. Mom would be starting her new job on Monday. The plan was to transfer our belongings to the new place after she got off work from her new job.

Mom couldn't spend another day sharing a bed with Rob and Gina, so she was going to take us to see Granny and Papa. At first, I thought this was a good thing, but the secret was that she was having difficulty leaving Rob the longer they continued to share a bed. The only change she wanted was for Gina to return to Guam.

11. Daddy's Girl

As we left Wichita Falls city limits, Mom asked me to light a cigarette for her while she was driving. I didn't know how to light a cigarette, so I held a cigarette with one hand and used the other to flick the lighter. The cigarette wouldn't light. It only burned the cigarette paper occasionally.

Mom blurted, "Wow, you weren't lying when you told Rob you didn't smoke. Put the cigarette to your lips and suck while you light it."

I took a puff of the cigarette and lit it for her. I began to cough as the smoke entered my lungs and passed the lit cigarette over to her. Mom's face was flushed with stress the entire hour's drive to Denton. Instead of seeing my grandparents, we took a detour to see my dad. We hadn't seen him since he took us from Mom sometime around my fourth-grade year.

He knocked on our door, and I answered, wearing nothing but my underwear as the spider had rewired me. I invited Dad inside while I was cooking Ramen for lunch. Mom came home soon after he arrived, and he asked to take us with him for the night. She consented, claiming she would love a night off. We got dressed and went to see where Dad lived. At the time, he lived in a one-bedroom apartment with his girlfriend and her son, Jackson, who was a year younger than Orion. The first week we lived as a family. We were prohibited from eating ramen unless covered in chili or tuna (which I found disgusting). He desired only the best for us. Dad wanted to know if Rob had ever touched or done anything wrong to Orion or me. His sister, Sarah, wanted to know so they could plan a way of hurting him the way he had us. Sarah rode shotgun while Dad drove, and I sat in the back seat with Orion. I lied and said nothing ever happened.

Dad began to sputter, "That's bull... whatever."
Sarah agreed, "I know he did. It doesn't matter if you tell us or not. Both of you act differently, like you've been beaten and locked in a cage. We'll get to the bottom of it, like it or not."
Dad took us to the circus, and I had the opportunity to ride a giant elephant. I also rode a donkey and pet some farm animals. It wasn't Orion's cup of tea. He enjoyed the circus show and clowns, the parts I didn't like so well. When getting ready to leave, Orion was first to try to get in Dad's truck. Dad's girlfriend put her leg up to kick him. Her son was spending the weekend with her sister, and she felt a bit bitter resentment towards Orion since he was Dad's biological son, instead of her son being treated as his child as he did before our arrival. I stood in the way to protect Orion. She smiled and got in the truck, pretending nothing had happened. Because of his girlfriend's jealousy, Dad no longer wanted us to stay at his place. I didn't want to stay with Dad anymore anyways. Jackson woke me up the last night that we stayed with Dad. He stood with my head between his feet as I slept. He had nothing but his underwear on, waking me up, shouting, "Suck it! Sissy, you hear me? Suck it!"
It's what the wrestlers on TV did. His mom apologized, but I didn't want to see that little kid anymore. I didn't care if it was a wrestling move. That's not what it felt like.
I had difficulty going back to sleep as I tried to remove the image replaying in my head. Isn't it strange, the more you want an idea out of your head, the more it repeats itself?

The following day, we were taken to Grandmama's house and stayed for a few days until she demanded that Dad take Orion back to his house, although I was welcome to stay as long as I liked. I visited for a few more days with Grandmama, but Sarah came to get me to help take care of Orion. I'm not sure what was so tricky about him to everyone else, but I didn't mind.

I was curious to see where Sarah lived. I met my little cousin, Hannah, and stayed in her room with her, sleeping on the floor while she slept in her crib. I watched her while Sarah and her boyfriend smoked weed in the living room. I never saw it. I just recognized the smell. The one time I came out of Hannah's room, I saw the metal tin they kept it in, hiding it quickly before I could see. I just wanted to see what the skunk smoke looked like. I was shooed back to my shared room with Hannah and watched her until I fell asleep. It was relaxing sleeping in a room with a baby. She was very cheerful and had curious, big brown eyes. She was always sitting in my lap, wanting me to play with her and her toys. I understood. When I was little, I always wanted someone to play with me. I had a reflexive mothering instinct for her, even though she just needed a babysitter sometimes. Sarah always came when Hannah cried and was the one to change her. Maybe it was the willingness that was different. I never had a little girl forced upon me. Taking care of her was optional, but I did it willingly.

We stayed with Sarah for two weeks until the police showed up, banging incessantly on the door until it was answered. We were taken to the police station in the back of a police car.

Mom had placed a missing children's report and was setting up custody with her lawyer as she prepared for divorce from Dad. He obviously didn't want us. He never came to visit after he left us with Grandmama. I couldn't say I missed him. He was just the same as before. How do you miss a beast that can't seem to transform into a man? At the divorce hearing, Grandmama claimed it would be best if my brother and I were separated because I would tell him the scariest stories I could imagine before he drifted off to sleep. I was a terror to him, and they would take me so I couldn't scare him anymore. It was a ploy to get custody over me and give back my brother to Mom as they wanted.

We arrived at Grandmama's house, where Dad stayed. Grandma and Grandpa weren't home, but Dad was there. Dad seemed just as surprised at our arrival as I was.

He noticed Orion immediately, but didn't speak to me for at least an hour. I sat alone on the couch as Dad talked to Mom as he held Orion in the kitchen. I suppose he forgot about me when he asked Mom, "So, who's that hot chick on the couch? Is she your friend? Does she want to come with us?"

My mom laughed as she raised an eyebrow, "That hot chick is your daughter. It's Annie."

His brows crowded together, confused, as he exclaimed, "No way. You've got to be kidding!"

She repeated, "No. That is your daughter. Did you think I only bought Orion?"

He looked down and embarrassed and shook his head. He smiled as he looked at me and walked into the living room where I sat.

He grinned, "Oh my goodness, Annie, it's you. Why didn't you say anything? I didn't recognize you. You've gotten so big. You're all grown up now."

I shrugged my shoulders as I began to stand up. "You didn't seem to notice me," I said.

He scoffed, as if I were wrong, and hugged me in his big arms.

Orion and I spent the weekend at Grandma and Grandpa's house while Mom and Dad rented a hotel room to have some time alone with one another. After the weekend came to a close, Mom came back and loaded us in her car. She informed us that we wouldn't be turning to Wichita Falls or living in the new apartment. We'd be staying in Denton in a three-bedroom apartment, and she was getting back together with Dad.

Mom needed an immediate replacement for Rob, so she wouldn't be tempted to stay with him. We moved into a large apartment where I had my own big empty room. Orion's room was next to mine, across from my parents. The space at the apartment was at least double the size of the house in Wichita Falls.

The living room and kitchen were always available. There was no room to walk through to get to either. Everything was becoming 'normal'.

It was an immediate improvement, even with none of our things there.

Dad picked up a couch, three television sets, a few

dressers, and some bedding he had bought at a garage sale. It gave us enough to begin to make the empty apartment feel more like a home, especially the living room. He promised to buy us each a bed soon.

Mom had to take a trip back to Wichita Falls to get our things. All we had with us were two sets of clothing, each that had already been worn.

While she was gone, I sat in the living room with Dad as he set up the TV. Once he had completed the task, he sat beside me on the couch.

He cleared his throat and looked over at me as he said, "So, tell me about Rob."

"He was fine," I vapidly replied.

There was no use in dragging out the truth. It was over. The truth had already been given and denied by Mom. Dad stared me down with his green eyes burning through me.

I stuttered, "Something happened, but I made Mom... Mom said I made it up. I got confused."

He smiled and cocked his head to the side, growling encouragingly, "That's bullshit, and you know it. If you don't know it, know that I know it. Come on now, what really happened? Tell me, and I'll believe you. Keep talking that bullshit, and I'll have to side with your mom. I don't want to, believe me. I've hated that cock-sucker from the very beginning. I called him the devil to his face. I called him out on it. I knew that bastard was evil. I just... couldn't stop her. I couldn't keep her from leaving me, leaving us, taking you. She wouldn't stay"

I smiled, "Me too. I never liked him, even when I first met him... So you promise you'll believe me... and not tell Mom I told you?"

He nodded dramatically, his green eyes practically glowing.

I told him everything. I told him more than was in my dairies but less than everything. It would take me many more years, more than a decade, to be able to do that. It all started with one person until I told the world, at least whoever is reading this book, you are the world in a single soul.

When I finished, Dad's eyes were bloodshot red, and the green glow almost protruded out of them. He had been nodding his head like a bobblehead until I stopped speaking. When I finished, he put his hands together to pray and placed his eyes upon his thumbs. The rage inside of him swirled around like the winds of a heavy thunderstorm.

He stood up suddenly, throwing his hands down to his sides until they began flailing around dramatically as he paced beside me and explosively repeated, "That's bullshit! That's mother fucking bullshit! That sick fuck!"

His hands were shaking from rage.

He looked at me and rhetorically asked, "How could your mother not believe you?"

He took a breath and sat back down as I felt anxious about how boisterous he was being.

As he sat next to me, his voice dropped back down, "It's bullshit, is what it is. I'm sorry... I'm sorry you had to live like that for that long, both you and Orion."

He tried to contain his rage as he said, "That piece of shit. Oh.. just wait. Just wait until your mother comes back. I'm telling her what I think about her allowing that sick fuck to live another day. I'm... I'm not mad at you, Ann... Storm. I just can't help but be pissed she continued for so long after I told her... I told her that's what he'd do. It's fucking ridiculous."

I muttered, "Please don't tell Mom I told you. Just leave it alone. It's done now."

He grinned with his glowering eyes, "Oh honey, I may not keep my promises, but I most definitely keep my word. Just try and stop me. You won't be able to."

Mom returned the next day around noon.

Had she spent the night with her spider? She had only rekindled her relationship with Dad to recover from the loss of her owner. In her mind, she had stopped the worst from happening when she asked permission to break up with him. Was she hoping he would say no, that he would be better? Even if he had lied, it probably would've been enough to keep her by his side for at least another month until she revealed the real issue. Or if Gina decided to leave. I can't say there was anything about him that any woman could want, let alone two women simultaneously. I saw no positive qualities within the spider. Instead, Rob said yes, that she was allowed to leave. After he had been seen for the monster he actually was.

How could any mother want him around their children?

Mom was a slave first and a mother second is the only explanation I can conjure.

Every girl loves a bad boy, right? I don't think that saying goes for the kind of evil he is.

Do you want to know the best way to get over a man? Fill yourself up with someone else instead. Preferably someone familiar that may feel wronged by you so they can hate-fuck you the only way you can feel it.

I felt bad about these thoughts and my confession when she arrived home with my favorite stray tabby kitten, that I had named Boy.

Mom chimed as she walked in, "Look here what I found, sweetheart. He was up a tree as I was pulling out to leave. It took me an hour to get him down. Rob helped me. But see, isn't he cute? Don't you... do you remember him?"

I smiled and bowed my head in shame when she placed him in my arms. "He's perfect," I confessed, "Thank you. I'm sorry. I told Daddy while you were gone. I didn't…."

Dad took mom by the arm, forcefully dragged her into their room, and slammed the door.

I paced my room nervously. *What had I done? It was so stupid! Why couldn't I just let it go? If she breaks up with Dad, she would just go to Rob. Dad believed me, but why even tell him? Just because he asked? Because I wanted someone to hate Rob as much as I did?*

Tears began to fall upon my face.

Yes! That's exactly what I wanted. I wanted him to be seen as a monster, just as I knew he was. Nobody could believe it. I just wanted someone to believe it. I just wanted to be honest for a change. I just... Why did he have to fight with her about it? It was over.

My brain felt like it was melting inside my skull from all the stress. The thoughts wouldn't stop flowing like an angry river leading to a waterfall; only the river was lava.

The cat was just a present to keep my mouth shut. It just came too late. Rob had helped get the cat down. I don't want anything that bastard touched. I looked at Boy and let the thoughts rush away. I watched him curl and stretch on the carpet, looking at me for attention. I began to pet him. His purr was loud, like a helicopter. I saw unconditional love staring into his eyes, my sense of calm. I renamed him, as 'Boy' was no name for a companion. He had the eyes of a lion, wide and outlined heavily in black. His fur was lighter than the average tabby, reflecting white and tan in the sun. Leos are lions, so he would be my Leo.

I could hear my parents fighting from my room, the sound echoing off the walls of all the empty spaces. I was too distracted in my own world of self-blame and cat-naming to hear it before.
"...We just went to dinner and had a few drinks. We were just catching up," Mom explained. Dad bellowed, "Catching up on what? His dick? You left him less than a week ago. That's absolute bullshit, and you know it! Hold on...let me ask..." I heard the door to my parent's room open, and my door opened immediately afterward. Dad peeked in the doorway and politely inquisitioned, "Hey, is this a bad time? Cause I've got a question to ask you." I replied, "No, that's fine. What did you wanna ask me?" He said, "So your mother said she spent the night with that bastard Rob, but she didn't sleep with him, didn't share a bed with him, even though she was gone all night long. Do you believe that shit?" Quid pro quo. I asked, "Where did she say she slept then?" "This bitch said she slept on the couch. What's up with that?" I smiled a smirk and took a breath as I shrugged my shoulders, "Yeah, man. It was a pretty comfy couch. I used to sleep on it when Rob wasn't home since I didn't have a bed. She probably did." He shook his head playfully in disappointment. I

didn't rile him up more like he had desired. *We didn't own a couch at the old house.* I wasn't about to tell him that. Dad went back to his room to finish the argument with Mom. I could tell a pretty good lie for a kitten. I no longer felt guilty for letting her come home to the madness.

I began getting the things Mom had brought from the old house out of her car, although there really wasn't all that much to retrieve. Eight black bags were sitting in her car's truck, and a few more were in the back seat. I brought all the bags upstairs to the apartment within a few trips. I wasn't sure what was what, so I thought it best to leave them alone and wait for instruction. It couldn't have taken more than an hour to gather what she had in bags. It was all clothes and bathroom items. I shook my head and went back to my new room with Leo.

I found some lotion in one of the dressers Dad had gotten from a garage sale, so I started painting my room with it. The smell of fresh paint was strong, so I was working on covering the odor up when Mom knocked on my bedroom door.

Mom asked softly, "Hey, baby girl. Are you busy? Would you maybe want to take a walk with me? I was going to walk to the gas station. I'd really like it if you came along,"

She hadn't asked me to walk with her since I was a little girl, so I happily accepted while remaining cautious. She had just come home to an argument, so I wasn't sure how to feel about going for a walk with her. We walked silently through the streets of the apartment complex before coming to a field across from the gas station. We talked on the way back about what Rob had done to me, and she would take me to make a statement at the police station in the morning.

I gave my statement as best I could. My mom watched from behind the invisible glass.

After it was done, the officer whispered to my mom, "There's nothing we can really do with this. I'm sorry. It'll just be her word against his once filed. I only hope this gave your daughter some closure, at least."

Mom whispered back, "It's okay. I don't think it happened

anyway."

Mom looked over at me, realizing I had heard them, since I was only standing by the desk beside them a few feet away.

Neither one of them whispered very well. She mouthed the words, "I'm sorry." I followed behind her to her car, knowing nothing had changed. The one person in this world that needed to believe me never would. She only did what she was told. My pain, sorrow, and story had no effect on her. She was still in love with Rob. My heart was beginning to fall out of love with her.

The following week, after Mom got home from work, she attempted suicide. Dad wanted me to talk to her as she sat in the closet on the premise of giving her something to live for, but I couldn't.

*All I could think was back to the past. I had threatened suicide with a butcher knife held firmly to my wrist because she told me to talk to Rob about an erotic poem I had written. She wanted proof I was still a virgin and wanted him to check. The idea was enough to wish I was dead. The last thing on Earth I wanted to do was talk to **him** about it. It wasn't for anyone to read, but no one could stay out of my notebooks. I held the knife to my wrist, tears streaming down my face.*

She only said, "go ahead, do it," as she watched me, unable to slice open my veins and let the blood pour.

I walked into her room, into her closet, where she sat behind clothes hung up with hangers.

Had she tried to hang herself from the clothes rack? Did she take a handful of pills? Was she going to stab herself with a butcher knife?

I never asked.

I walked hesitantly from my room into theirs.

The only words I uttered while in the closet were, "That's stupid. Why don't you go ahead and do it?" Mom's words were coming out of my mouth.

She heard nothing of my pain. Why should I be bothered by hers?

Dad laughed as I left her in the closet and returned to my

room.

It was one of the ugliest things that I have ever done.

It was exactly what Dad wanted me to do. He wanted more power over her, and it was easiest to gain it when she was hopeless. After all, his love was still negging.

He knew exactly how I felt. It's why he called on me instead of Orion. My brother would have been sympathetic.

My dad berated her with insincere comments, "Oh, poor baby. Here comes the pity party. I'm so sad. I guess I'll just kill myself. Poor pity you. That's all there ever is."

After hearing him make fun of her, I only began feeling bad about what I had said.

It was a terrible day.

12. Chemical Madness

The following week I gave Mom a drawing I had made in art class. I was incredibly proud of it. Our class had been instructed to combine the letters of our names into a piece of art. I chose to use the name Andromeda. The artwork that came from my name was exquisite.

It looked like the satanic star and the anarchy sign fused together, adorning a wizard hat and scythe. It was macabre and elegant, abstract yet fully formed.

A few days after giving it to her, sonar screams screeched from her room. She claimed a demon had erupted from my artwork. It was a dark shadow wizard wielding a scythe, just as my drawing had depicted. Mom claimed that she had locked it in the closet so it wouldn't kill her.

She rolled up my artwork, sealed it with a zip tie, and burned it to exorcize the demon.

I had conjured a demon to kill her by giving her my artwork... I wondered if it had been true. Was I truly capable of conjuring demons? Was I the secret ruler of the dark universe?

Leo sat upon my box-set TV and stayed awake at night to watch the shadows beneath my bedroom door, his body hunched defensively anytime a shadow passed. I thought he was adorable, wanting to defend me from whatever may be outside. The aggravating part was he *refused* to cuddle. He would not be brought to share my bed, even when I tried to force him to understand the comfort. His place was hunched upon the warm heat behind the static screen of the TV, keeping watch as I slept.

Evil was brewing, but it was not my doing. I am not the

dark overlord. I wasn't even the evil that resided in our home. Our home was being haunted, but not by any monster I had ever known.

There are substances in this world that can bring the demon out in almost anyone. There is no conjuring involved. It is brewed in bathtubs or vats, stirred cautiously, by at-home chemists. Once found, bought, or stolen, all that has to be done is inhale it, and it will take over your life. The only equipment needed is a tiny fish bowl attached to a glass straw and preferably a torch lighter.

The price?

It's only worth the price of your home, worldly positions, sanity, family, and any love you have ever known. More money must be made because it consumes all and more. The more you have, the more you need. Chemical intoxication is no different than the real world we all live in. The only difference is instead of random wants and needs, it is a singular obsession.

Mom worked a three-day shift at *Denny's*, taking off one day between her twenty-four-hour shifts to keep the chemicals flowing in and the bills paid.

Mom's last delusion ended any bond that may have grown between my father and I.

To be honest, he had become my hero. We talked most of the day each day and went everywhere together. He wasn't employed, so he could do the things that mom couldn't as she worked tirelessly. I just wanted a friend. Apparently, our time together didn't mean that much to him.

My parents rekindling their love had been challenging. He was unnerved at her for ever leaving him, especially for the likes of the spider. She had difficulties recovering from the heart back from losing her master for the safety of her children. It led to countless arguments.

Mom came home from work after one of her three-day work binges and slammed the door as soon as she walked in.

She began to slur, "I know what you two are up to. Believe me, I know. Ain't no secrets here that I don't know. You're plotting to leave me and run off, run away together. You don't think I know, but I know. What?... You two are fuckin' while I spend all my time at work. I work my ass off, and 'ere you are off fuckin' in the house that I pay for. Well, it won't work. Nope, not while I'm around. You might like her tight ass now, but I'm the original model."

I began to form the word what but my mouth only made it as far as, "wha-" I could barely understand anything she said.

Dad hushed, "Don't worry, we'll get all this sorted out."
He took Mom by the arm and walked her to their room. She was in dire need of a nap. After a couple hours, she woke up from her slumber and tapped on my door.
She asked me to go into the living room to talk to her.

Mom mumbled, "So I was told when I came in earlier. I accused you of doing a horrible thing. I accused you and your dad of sleeping together. I really don't remember, but that's what he said. So I just wanted to let you know that I don't think that's true. I've just been working a lot. Too much, really. I'm not sure what I was thinking. I don't even remember saying it. I just want you to know that I'm sorry."

I pondered for a moment, unaware that all of her slurs were actual words. I said the best thing I knew to be accurate, "You're crazy. You've always been crazy. It's okay. It's you. I wasn't really sure what you were saying anyway." I said it with a smile, so it was spoken warmly, but I didn't know anything else to say. As she stood there, confused, I whispered, "Don't worry, I won't tell the asylum. It's the forbidden word."

She began to smile as she walked back to her room feeling better than she had before.

I began to wonder who these new friends were that came to the apartment to spend time in my parent's room. What did they want to know if they had more of? Had my parents started some strange cult? Were they swingers? Why did they always come in pairs?

My curiosity got the best of me. Leo tried to stop me, corralling me back into our room, but I had to find out what was going on, so I jumped past him and tried to tip-toe around the corner to my parent's room.

Were they conjuring demons and blaming me? I would not be their scapegoat.

It took multiple attempts to cross the intersection from my room to theirs without being seen.

I finally saw the smoke coming from a single tiny fish bowl held in Dad's hands as he blew out a thin cloud of smoke. A little bag of blue rocks laid in front of them on the table.

Were they all smoking table salt? Silica? Blue bath salt maybe? Or were they just trying to smoke rocks they found outside?

I couldn't be sure. Dad rushed me to my room, explaining it was steroids. He claimed, "...You don't even have to work out for the steroids to work. You can just smoke them and stay up, and it does the work for you."

I smiled as I said, "Yeah... I don't think that's how you do steroids, Pop. Nice try"

I walked away, leaving him with nothing to say. I didn't know what steroids were, but from what I understood, I thought they had to be injected. Mostly it just felt like all the times he had convinced me that I had eaten Bambi or Bugs Bunny or whatever else he wanted to come up with to trick me. I was too old to be fooled now. I craved the truth because the secrets were overtaking our lives.

My Leo found a rock in the carpet and ate it. I don't know why there was a crystal lying in my room. Maybe it was swept in. My poor Leo was never quite the same. He was angrier, even more, protective than he was before. No one was to trespass in my room, or he would hiss and growl at them until they were gone. He barely liked to be pet anymore. He'd cower his ears down as if it were painful or thought I would hurt him instead of petting him.

Leo was pacing the door when I returned from my trip in the hall. He was terrified, nervous, and unable to protect me outside our room. My room was the only place where Leo felt safe. He was my guardian angel, and felt lost if he could not protect me.

A week later, Mom took me on another walk to the gas station a week later. On the walk back, she let out the thoughts that had been trapped silently.

She said, "I think you'd be better off in a foster home or adopted if you can. If CPS comes like they did before, tell them you need to be there. I can't... I don't feel like I can take care of you anymore. I can't protect you. I don't know how. Just tell them that, and you should be safe."

I walked up the stairs to the apartment, trailing ahead of her without regard for the distance between us. I had nothing to say to her as she attempted to release me from her custody.

My parents' bickering turned into nights filled with laughter echoing loudly in the apartment. Mom only worked mornings and some afternoon shifts, taking off to spend time with Dad and their new mysterious friends. Dad and I barely associated anymore, not since Mom accused us of sleeping together.

I didn't mind being alone anymore. I could come and go from my room as I wished, but I usually chose to stay cooped up with Leo. Sometimes I'd go on a date with Ty with his parents playing chaperone.

I got back together with Ty, my boyfriend from kindergarten, on one of my previous outings with Dad. He wanted to visit Ty's dad and thought I might like to see an old friend. Dad allowed us to date as long as we didn't have sex. Sex was new to me, so it wasn't a big deal. We could still go on dates and make out in his room. For a while, I chose to obey Dad's rule even when I was pressured by Ty to break it. Instead, alone in my room, I used the condoms I was given by the gynecologist on one of the visits to cover my fingers while I masturbated. It was almost as good as the real thing.

Afterwards, I was too embarrassed to walk into the kitchen to throw the condom away. I'd throw it behind my bed, expecting myself to retrieve it later and put it in the trash. I forgot for about a month until they all piled up and Dad came looking in my room while I was at school.

I arrived home to Dad sitting in his room, peering out into the hall, cursing under his breath. This wasn't a new occurrence until I noticed the door of my room was open, and Leo stood in the doorway, poofed up like he had been fluffed

in the dryer. He looked rigid, staring at Dad as if this stare-down had been going on for hours, and Leo forgot how to calm down.

I cooed, "Leo...Leo. Whatcha doin' buddy?"

Leo cuddled against my legs and the door frame, simmering down his fight mode. I went to close my door, and Dad growled, "Don't you close that door, young lady! You're grounded! There are no more closed doors."

I didn't ask why. I just went into my room to lay on the floor and stare at Leo while listening to music.

Dad shouted from the next room, "I've got your boyfriend on the phone. I've got a few questions for that boy."

He had a very loud thirty-minute conversation with Ty, with plenty of bullshits thrown into the mix, until his voice got quieter as he said, "so she didn't use all the condoms with you? I'm so sorry. Let me get down to the bottom of this."

He made Ty cry, thinking I was having consistent sex with another guy that snuck into my room at night.

Dad stomped into my room and growled, "You wanna know what I found today? Take one guess. It was behind your bed."

I sat up from lying on the floor while Leo stood straight by my side.

I replied, "Condoms." *I had nothing to hide. It was just a bit embarrassing, which is why I never threw them away, worried I might be asked what was in my hand.*

Dad was overcome with anxiety as he rubbed his hands on his pockets to dry off his sweating palms. He was riddled with confusion with my reply being so short. He tried to think of how to talk about something he had no desire to talk about.

He took a breath as he asked, "So who... what... Who has been sneaking into your room at night? I had one simple rule, and you broke it. Did you think I wouldn't find out? You've been caught. Now fess up."

I smiled, trying not to laugh at how serious Dad was, "Caught what? Masturbating? My hand keeps sneaking into my room at night. With these nails," I held up my hand to display my long fingernails, "it helps to use a condom, so I don't scratch myself down there."

His complexion went pale. He turned around to leave, then faced me, repeating this process several times, walking in a dizzy semi-circle.

Finally, he looked at me and stammered, "That's bull-... that... I'll be right back. I need to have a talk with your mother."

Mom and Dad talked for another half hour until it was determined that I had told the truth. Dad returned to my room and apologized, "I'm sorry that I thought you... uh, well, you know. There's a whole huge mess of condoms back there that you need to clean up. I know it's wrong to go through your room. It's an invasion of privacy, and I am guilty of that, so forgive me. I was just worried, you know. I worry about you, especially since you're dating a boy. You wouldn't be allowed to date if I didn't know him, but he's a good kid. So are you. You should call him and tell him I made a mistake. I'll vouch for you. I shouldn't have called before talking to you about it. I was just so sure that's what you were doing. But first, clean that mess up. You know what, I'll call him again when you're through, so there won't be any problems between you two."

Dad spoke to me even less after his awkward discovery. It was like we all lived in separate homes in the confines of the apartment.

The only time I heard his voice was when he was in his room with the door opened, chanting, "They're in there. I can feel it. I have to get them out," as he dug holes in his arm with a pair of tweezers.

It was a recurring all-day procedure. Occasionally he would pull a sweat gland out of his arm, which looked like a thin, white worm. Pulling one out only encouraged him to look for more. "I can see it squirm. Sick! They're everywhere," he said to himself.

I never asked why worms had dug into his veins or why he didn't go to a doctor instead of performing this surgery himself. Burrowing into his skin was his full-time job. Roughly, he worked the same amount of hours as Mom, but she got paid for her hours, unlike him. She worked tirelessly to keep a roof over our heads. I was under the impression she did anyway until a notice appeared on our front door. Mom made three hundred dollars per day working double shifts as a waitress, but it was not enough to pay for a place to live and sustain their meth habit. Rent hadn't been paid in two months, half of the time, we had been living in the apartment. A lock would be placed outside the door if not paid within a week. We were no longer welcome to stay in the apartment and were required to leave.

When I asked Dad about it, he replied, "There must be some mistake. They got the wrong house."

After asking Mom, she said, "Yeah, I'm going to try and have it paid soon. If not, we'll have to find a new place to stay, and I'm sure they won't allow pets."

The lock was placed on the outside door, but since Dad was always home, we stayed an additional two weeks before I had to give up Leo.

I asked Ty to watch him, but his sister was allergic, so he was their outdoor cat for a time. I missed him because he was gone, but I missed him even more when I visited him. He treated me like a stranger, refusing to come to me. It broke my heart too much to see that the best protector I ever had no longer knew who I was. Since I rarely had the chance to visit him, Ty's parents gave him away. Waking up without him sleeping on my static-filled tv in my room made living in a two-bed motel room even worse.

There were two working television sets, but I didn't care to watch tv. I just wanted my cat. The one time I had an interest in watching something, Dad told me it was inappropriate as he pulled a sheet across our bed, leaving us with no tv and unallowed from getting out of bed as he continued watching it on both tv sets. He was turning into a colossal douchebag.

In the motel, there was no kitchen or rooms besides the shared bedroom and the undersized bathroom. My parents placed a permanent sheet between our two beds, only about two feet apart. If we crossed the sheet without announcing that we needed to get by, we would get yelled at and made to go back over until a time was deemed appropriate for us to cross. I shared a twin-sized bed with Orion, who wanted to cuddle and occasionally wet the bed. There was no place on the floor to sleep to avoid this from happening. Otherwise, I would've happily slept on the floor to prevent awkward cuddles and golden showers.

I began to feel animosity towards everything. The motel didn't have a fridge or a way to save food if we had any. Dad had a stash of potato chips but seldomly shared, often eating them up in a single day. Mom's income at *Denny's* was spent on the motel room and their chemical addiction. The sheet had been placed so they could smoke dope and have sex whenever they liked. Trying to sleep with the sounds of Mom moaning and Dad grunting while saying dirty things to Mom was near to impossible.

Any comment or response to anything said or done at any time in the confines of their sheet was a reason to be yelled at.

If we didn't respond while being spoken to from the other side of the sheet, it was also a reason to be reprimanded. There was no winning here. It was much like living with Rob if only the physical abuse was taken out of the picture.

Going to school was my only escape until I arrived home with a B minus in math on my report card. That was unacceptable as an A student. Dad punished me by requiring me to study from when I arrived home until it was time for bed. The more I stared at the book, the more dramatically my grades dropped.

Until Dad growled, "Obviously, you're not doing the work. Study harder! It's unacceptable. You're smarter than this. You need to participate in sports. Any child of mine needs to play a sport. Get noticed by a college, get a scholarship"

Apparently, I wasn't that intelligent because I continued to fail more and more classes, even gym. I was terrible at sports. I had no interest in them. I was on the brink of failing eighth grade.

Such a dramatic change in my grades warranted a wellness check from CPS. A warning was given days before their arrival, so Dad went out and bought a cooler, filled it with ice, and filled it with his favorite ready-to-eat foods consisting primarily of barbecue, pre-made mac and cheese, and bologna. The night the case worker arrived, Dad had ordered pizza and took the sheet down that separated our beds. The caseworker that came over would have been perfect for a family that was just going through a difficult financial time, but I couldn't help but wonder if it might not be better if we were taken somewhere else. It seemed like we were always getting put in some kind of a cage. With an unrealistic look at what an ordinary day in our life looked like, my parents were given a pass.

A case worker showing up would have been a wake-up call for any parent to get their life back on track, but Dad had never actually been a parent. It was more like acting a part in a movie and quitting when it was inconvenient for him. He had three more kids who had only met him on a few occasions. He didn't have to hide who he was while living with Mom, unlike living with his parents, where he was expected to be on his best behavior.

Mom tried to stop smoking from the glass pipe, but upon returning home from a double shift, she came home, crying, "I'm tired. I'm just so tired. I don't want to do this anymore."

Thinking up a solution, Dad carried her into the bathtub and shut the bathroom door as she cried. He returned to his bed to grab his gear bag and locked the bathroom door behind him.

From the hollow bathroom, Mom pleaded, "No, I don't want it. You can't make me. No! Stop! You're hurting me."

"Stop fighting. You'll feel better in no time," Dad hushed.

An audible tapping of skin sounded. Dad muffled, "This will only hurt a little. Try to enjoy it."

Mom screamed out in pain, and a rubber band snapped afterwards. Mom didn't fight back, but she wasn't a willing participant.

How was he any better for her than Rob? This was just another form of brainwashed control. We lived just as we had in the beginning with the spider, trapped in a cage.

Is a prison any better if there isn't a lock? If the cage is only contained by a door and a sheet? Does the idea of having freedom take away the suffocation of the mind? I won't say it's worse, but a bird that believes it can fly will try. However, a bird that loses its sense of freedom and forgets that it can fly will go insane. Birds are capable of losing their mind, just as people do. *You're crazy; you've always been crazy,* repeated in my mind. I felt like Alice plummeting down an endless rabbit hole.

By the time I believed things could only get worse from here, my parents were both sent to jail while Orion and I were at school. Oddy enough, it had nothing to do with the possession of drugs. Dad went to jail with felony charges of failing to pay child support on all five of his kids.

Mom went to jail for a more noble cause. She had been writing 'hot checks' to ensure we were fed at least once per day.

Mom only ate a few bites of food per day and probably would

have had less had she not wanted to eat with everyone else. Dad spent his day at home, consuming more than all three of us. Mom had written a bad check each day for three months.

The police came when a warrant was placed on her, giving her a misdemeanor. Dad was the bonus catch, committing a felony of failure to pay child support for all five of his kids.

My respect for Mom grew instantly, only now understanding how hard she tried to take care of us, even though she initially failed to give us the better life she hoped for.

Addiction is not as easy as simply stopping, although beginning the process is as easy as obtaining and consuming a substance. Addiction rewires the brain the same way a mental disorder does. The brain's chemistry will never be the same. Once an addict, always an addict. The only way to make it stop is genuinely wanting to stop with every ounce of willpower you have. It can't be forced or asked for. It has to be desired by the addict. Even then, the withdrawal of the chemical's absence is often too much to bear. It takes infinite self-discipline and patience to come through it, resisting all temptations. It's not an easy task. Giving in is so much easier, especially when it's the one thing that keeps you motivated. It's impossibly difficult to overcome, but not impossible. It can only be done if you believe in yourself and become your own hero.

13. Charity Case

Grandmamma stood waiting at the bus stop for us to return to the motel after being released from school for the day. I had never seen this glamorous woman cry, but tears all but fell from her glittering eyes. Her eyes looked like they were made of water, two small ponds with lily pads sitting in their center. What made her glamorous wasn't her clothes. I never saw her in a dress or wearing gaudy jewelry. It was her demeanor, posture, and how her nails remained perfectly manicured, painted mauve no matter what day it was, as if it was a natural beauty mark.

Grandmama took us to her home, a beautiful white brick home with a rose and rock garden out front. A pine tree loomed over the fence line. It was too pretty of a home to actually live in. It felt like a tour through a dollhouse. It was strange to think people lived there, especially a child, in such an immaculate home. My uncle was their adopted son, an eight-year-old boy my grandparents had been gifted with from my aunt. My uncle wasn't expected to live very long and had to take many medications to remain healthy.

Grandmamma opened her home to us for a couple of days until Mom could be bailed out of jail. I slept in grandma's bed, supposedly beside her, but I never saw her go to bed or knew when she woke up. I wondered if she ever slept or was some sort of secret vampire or a robot with flesh-colored skin and realistic features. How did she recharge? Even machines need to rest. Her bed was too comfortable not to slumber in. Her blankets were filled with down feathers that crumpled like the sound of snow when it was laid upon. It was like sleeping in the fluffiest cloud.

Orion slept on the couch loaded with fuzzy blankets with

depictions of different *Disney* characters. He slept cozily in the living room, where Grandpa slept in his recliner nightly. It was strange that my grandparents slept in separate beds. Granny and Papa slept in the same one, even when they weren't happy together anymore.

Grandmama told me, "Girls sleep with girls, and boys sleep on their own."

Grandmama bailed Mom out of jail and brought her to us to give back her guardianship.

Grandmama said, "You don't have to take Annie if you need more time to figure this mess out. I would have bailed out my son, but his bail was too high to pay out. You put him there. You need to repay me for your bail, but find a way to get my son out. He doesn't belong there."

The thing about my grandparents is that they always treated me better than they did my brother, as if I were family and he was my half-brother or something. They were never unkind, but they preferred his time with them to be short. Whether it was because I was their first grandchild or because Orion had autism that caused him not to be treated as generously as me. I could stay as long as I liked, but Mom was bailed out to find a place for Orion to go. Was it his strange ticks? He often walked around biting his hand while wiggling his fingers in front of his face, which made him look much like a jumping spider moving its pedipalps around. He hummed and exclaimed randomly, but that was just his way. Often, at times it drove me crazy, but overall, it's what made him Orion. There is no single person alike with autism. It is a vast spectrum. Or was it because he peed the couch made into a bed. He learned how to use the toilet while we were there. He was getting better. My uncle and brother were around the same age, give or take a couple of years. He talked a lot but began speaking a few years late, so he constantly had a lot to say.

I chose to go with my mom. She didn't know where to go, but paying for the crime of making sure we didn't go hungry was enough to earn back some loyalty. I left my grandparent's beautiful home to try to make it in the world with my mom and brother.

We finally made our way to visit Papa. He initially greeted us warmly, although he was deep in his drink. Someone in the neighborhood had bought him his favorite bottle of whiskey..

Whiskey made him a bitter drunk. When Mom asked if we could stay with him for a while, he exclaimed with intransigence, "Not you! You are not welcome here. Not when you're with that no-good piece of shit, be he in jail or not. You chose him, not them kids. You can leave my grandbabies here. I'll take them. Give 'em to me. I'll do better than you ever could. You don't want them babies."

Mom hurried us back out the door and left before he said something he might regret.

Papa yelled, "You're nothing but trash, just like him! You'll never be nothing but a no-good junkie whore."

We drove off with nowhere to go.

Granny no longer lived with Papa. They didn't believe in divorce, so she moved in with her sister at my great-grandmother's house. Her sister lived there after their mom passed away. I had only met my great-grandmother a handful of times, but I had never met Granny's sister. Granny offered us the living room after mom called and asked if we could stay.

It was the only good thing that came from seeing Papa. Otherwise, Granny would have been difficult to find.

My great-grandmother's house was a white two-bedroom cottage. It wasn't half as fancy as Grandmama's place, but it was still better than staying in the motel.

Granny exacerbated the light of freedom. She no longer lived in an endless dungeon of her thoughts.
However, the longer we stayed, the less she seemed to glow like she did before we moved in.

We left after a few weeks to lessen her stress. The longer

we stayed, the more her sister complained of Mom inflating the phone bill, as she received calls from Dad in jail. Each week the bill went up two hundred dollars from all the calls from prison. There was no way for Granny to pay them, and her sister definitely wasn't going to waste money on these calls. Mom did the best she could to pay Granny back before we moved in with my uncle, Carl. Granny requested our leave when the stress was too much, as she was becoming exhausted trying to manage the chaos.

Every time the phone rang, I could feel my stomach twist in knots, causing a dizzy sickness of nausea.

All of her I love you, miss you, can't wait to see you, I'll wait for you, and all the schoolgirl giggles during the calls repulsed me. The phone was in the living room, so I couldn't help but hear all of it. Disgust wasn't felt because my parents were acting like teenagers or the fact that Dad was in jail. My feelings of repressed rage were beginning to come to the surface. My father was a narcissist incapable of love. Mom only said loving words to him out of neurotic guilt. She felt guilty, as if he went to jail because of her.. With his lack of presence over the years, she only asked for money to support the children he helped create. He didn't support us, so he went to jail. It was plain and simple. He hadn't taken care of us since living together again, even in the beginning. He was just looking for ammunition against Mom, and I gave it to him. Mom hadn't been the best mother in a long time, but she was there to keep us alive.

Increased love due to guilt isn't love. It's a harmful obsession. Emotions are a complex galaxy. Everyone has to find their way through. How emotions collide in such a way as if there are no lines around them is insanity. Love turns into hate, turns into guilt, increases love, brings upon sadness, and so on in a dizzy maze on repeat with no specific reason or order. Emotions bleed into one another so savagely that it's difficult to tell them apart. Apathy, however, is the opposite of all other emotions. Except in that case, apathy is a symptom of depression, so sometimes it's also a distant type of sadness. The sense of emotion is non (non-sense), but emotion is all that we can feel. (Not everyone. Some people can turn it off or lack the switch that turns emotion on at all, so they only feel what they perceive others would feel, if even that. A mask of a mind, a mask instead of a switch. While the rest of us flow tyrannically in a river of emotions. Is that sanity or madness?) There is a thin line between brilliance and insanity.

We moved in with my uncle And slept in his living room. At least he had two big couches. Orion had his own space in the back, equipped with toys and a private TV. Mom and I took a sofa each. My uncle was a disabled diabetic who had to have both of his legs amputated due to gangrene. His girlfriend had just left him to fend for himself. He needed someone to move in and take care of him.

He had to be taken to the hospital monthly to stay for a few days. He required blood and iron transfusions and to stay longer and be monitored for a few days. He needed help around the house, rides to his doctor's appointments and to the hospital, and someone to clean up the accidents that sometimes occurred. He even needed help bathing. He was helpless on his own, so he was thankful for our need for a place to stay. Mom never asked me to help, but occasionally I would cook.

I was consumed with everything I saw in my uncle's an eerily haunted house and the oddities it caused me to see. The off-white walls would turn a transparent shade of rose gold, being taken over with overgrown foliage with vines that grew up the walls that were turned to gray stone. Branches of trees tore through the ceiling, leaving massive holes for them to flourish. The sky above was crimson red, inhabiting a violet moon that could be seen through the side where the tree had torn through. The ceiling lay in shambles, leaving cracks running throughout, warning that it all could crash if only a strong enough breeze passed through.

Eyes surrounded me as I laid on the couch and tried to sleep. Bodies would replace Mom until she would disappear, being replaced by an old couple that took over the couch. I tried turning the other way so they couldn't stare at me, rolling the other way to face the back couch cushions, and even covered my face with the blanket that covered me. But I could still feel their gaze burning my skin until tiny glass-filled blisters formed. Waking the next morning after the haunting, my skin would be covered in red welts with the glass-filled bumps in the middle. The majority of the glass pustules were on my back, where I couldn't reach. Mom helped dig out the shards with a pair of tweezers for me, as they only felt better after the shards were taken out. Mom remarked, "This looks like meth. Do you think I should try to smoke it?" I'm not sure if she was being serious or joking. Either way, I replied, "I don't think that's a good idea. I don't think drugs are growing out of my body." Looking disappointed, she sighed, "You're probably right." I didn't want to know if she had ever tried it.

Mom had some of the same marks on her skin, although not as severe. Hers occurred on her arms and chest, with plenty of healthy skin in between the blisters. We laid on our couch beds at night, groaning, tossing, and turning, unable to get comfortable as the wounds burned unbearably at night. Mom openly smoked in the living room from her fish bowl, so the more time she was away, the more the chemical rash began to disappear.

The anti-meth ghosts were pleased with her absence.

Mom had not been looking for a job initially upon moving in, as she took care of my uncle full time, until his ex-girlfriend, Andrea, decided she lived there, and they had never broken up after a month.

Mom and Andrea did not get along well, to say the least.

Andrea felt as though she had been replaced. Hence, she took her jealousy out by making snide comments, talking down to Mom, and insisting we begin paying rent since my uncle was being taken advantage of by accepting labor in lieu of rent.

Mom ceased taking care of my uncle, as anything she helped with was done incorrectly, not fast enough, and certainly not enough to pay the rent we owed for staying.

Andrea often sabotaged dinner plans by eating all of the toppings Mom had bought for dinner, like an entire bag of cheese as Mom was making enchiladas.

Complaints were made since Mom couldn't finish the job on time because she had to return to the store when Andrea ate all the cheese, claiming she didn't know it was for dinner. She was just hungry, and it looked too good not to eat.

It was impossible to do anything with Andrea around. She didn't like anyone aside from Orion, who she pretended was her child.

14. Heartbreak and Lust

Occasionally I went on a date with Ty, but it seemed the more I gave him, the less he wanted me. I promised myself I wouldn't have sex until after my next birthday. Sometimes it was difficult waiting, especially when Ty would try to seduce me, but I held out until a week after turning fifteen.

He seemed to lose interest as the chase to have all of me was over. Once he obtained what he wanted regularly, he broke up with me for a girl he went to church with. She believed in God with him, unlike me. I even went to church with Ty just because he went, but it wasn't good enough. I had noticed something had changed the last time I went to church with him. The looks I received made me feel like an inconvenience, even though Ty was the one that had brought me there. He often invited a friend to his house after church to avoid my seduction. It wasn't as fun when the girl did the pressuring. In all actuality, he just wanted to be told no again. I had become too easy even though I had made him wait a year with continual pressure from him to give myself to him. The grass is always greener on the other side of the fence.

Maybe I was ugly naked, orgasmed too frequently, or was bad at sex? But how would he know? He was the one that was a virgin, supposedly. Maybe my addiction to it was unappealing. I turned from virgin to whore rather quickly, even though it wasn't my first time.

I cried for a week, especially when it seemed like he called more often to check in on me than he had the entire time we had been together. I didn't understand the game being played.

My aunt Sarah took me in for a couple of weeks to help me overcome the breakup. She allowed me to drink an entire pack of Smirnoff wine coolers per night while we drove around. She would often take me over to visit with her friends, who all smoked meth together, often in a circle around me. It seemed like every grown-up smoked dope.

I preferred sitting with them rather than sitting in a room alone with nothing to do or sitting in Sarah's truck for hours in the dark. I was offered the drug many times but never participated in smoking from the glass pipe.

She should meet up with men in random parking lots if she wasn't smoking with her friends. More often than not, they were married.

What better location than a car? There are no hotel receipts, it's free, and leaves no trace of infidelity.

I never watched. I just sat in the passenger seat of her little blue truck and drank my beers as the car beside me shook back and forth like a mechanical bull on wheels. Once, we stayed over at one of the men's apartments. They ordered pizza, and we ate, drank together, and watched scary movies on the television. I was handed a blanket to sleep on the couch, after which they started making out on the sofa beside me. I was happy when they went off to his bedroom before it went any further.

I had no interest in watching other people have sex. Sometimes it got a little annoying because anytime a boy showed interest in me, I was told no and given another beer. There was some strange hypocrisy going on. I was young, but I would've been allowed to smoke methamphetamines if I wanted, drink alcohol, watch Sarah have sex, and make out with different men every other day, but I was not allowed to be sexually active myself.

My body craved lust, as I had just gotten out of a relationship that had a lot in it at the end. I was a sex addict without permission to have sex. It doesn't make the feeling go away. If anyone should have understood, it was an addict. It only made me try to be a little secretive.

Sarah took me to the water park with her often, smoking a joint on the way there as she drove. Strangely, I was never offered to try it. I could've used a way to relax.

Instead, I was on the hunt. While she was sleeping on a float in the lazy river, I would sneak off to talk to boys. I even had sex in the main indoor pool with a boy my age, but I didn't find it enjoyable. It was meaningless and felt like a bird flapping underneath my bikini bottoms instead of intercourse. I felt nothing but waves of water splashing in my eyes uncomfortably.

Afterwards, the boy ghosted me. It was probably obvious that I didn't enjoy the act and it wasn't worth talking about.

I swore off boys my age after Ty and the awkward encounter at the waterpark. I began to see the men Sarah talked to as much more interesting targets of wanting to spread my lust.

After all, Mom taught me the best way to get over a man was to get under a new one. I didn't want them to hate-fuck me, but I felt less heartbroken when men showed interest in me.

Since I was so good at talking to men, Sarah often requested that I go ask them out for her. Initially, they'd show interest in me (*the fifteen-year-old wearing a skull bikini very well*) *until I told them I was asking for my aunt,* a rather obese blonde who only had a B-cup chest, so I never had any luck when I asked for her. I was a size three with a pair of C's, so I wasn't a good wingman. I can only imagine that it made the men I asked to feel like a prank was being played on them.

I worked a job painting a bowling alley with Sarah and a few of her male friends. One began flirting as soon as he saw me until Sarah told him whose daughter I was. He instantly said he had no idea and wished I were older.

I began to learn that age is only a number. If he hadn't known my mom, I'm sure we would've made some memories together.

All of her male friends were very attractive.

The one that was intimidated by my mom was by far the prettiest, having dark hair, tanned tattooed skin, and bright green eyes that were easily seen watching my every move. How he bit his lip as he stared made me want to tear off my clothes and make him forget who my mother was. *If only Sarah wasn't painting beside me.*

We worked for three days painting the walls of the bowling alley. Sarah stayed by my side, noticing how they looked at me, and even at times, came off as being jealous. We'd paint together, and a few times, she asked me why I had to wear such short shorts and a tank top every day we worked.

I replied, "It's just so hot in here. It's like a hundred degrees outside. It's even hotter in here with no AC"

That part was true, but I could've chosen a different outfit at times instead of the same pair of short jean shorts every day. The only thing that changed was my shirt. Working with a full, short-sleeved shirt was easier than a bouncy tank top.

One of her other friends, the contractor for the job, claimed I wore my shorts for him, which turned into a heated argument between him and Sarah. I was turning into jail bait in a hurry.

On the last day of work, I rode in her friend's truck, which he claimed was the only way Sarah would get paid for her days working. She drove behind us in his SUV on the way to his house. While we drove, he had a large bag of crystal meth sitting on the console between us. I was a bit worried he would get pulled over with him sitting it out in the open all the way to his house.

It was a personal test. He wondered if I would take meth as a payment even though he was told I didn't smoke it. He was curious if I did, and nobody knew it.

Once we got to his house, he handed me two large garbage bags of designer clothes. He sorted out his payment with Sarah while I dug through the clothes, admiring how pretty everything was. There were short lace dresses, tube tops, mini skirts, and thong underwear. I happily bartered my time for the entirety of the two bags. I never saw her cute friends again.

I wanted to, but I was never allowed to be alone with them.

Sarah gave away all of my cutest outfits to one of her friends and dropped me back off at my uncle's house the next day. I tried to protest, but she told me I had more than what I needed, and she had just gotten out of jail and needed clothes. I huffed as I left the room, feeling angry and betrayed.

I would've given some of my clothes away, but her friend had a full choice of my clothes, and I had no say. My favorite outfits were gone in a matter of minutes. Sarah encouraged it. I couldn't steal her well deserved attention wearing baggy clothes.

I thought she was my friend, but I guess Dad and her had more in common than I thought. She left me when I was inconvenient for her.

15. Transformation

Mom was working at a strip club as a server and was gone most of the time, as she worked nights and spent most of her free time with friends and going on dates, often spending the night if she didn't have to work. She only returned home to get ready for work, drop off groceries, and make dinner for all of us as long as Anna wasn't around. I didn't associate with anyone much, not even Orion or my uncle.

I spent most of my time outside watching the stray cats, sitting on the porch. It was my happy place. The house seemed less haunted since returning to it again. Most of the cats didn't allow me to pet them, but the prettiest long-haired Seal-point Siamese did. I was hesitant to give him attention, as he looked much like Sapphire, which was one of the few cats I despised. He had dusty white fur with charcoal markings on his tail, feet, and face. He smelled like a dumpster fire, but I didn't care. He let me hold and hug him as often as I liked as long as I gave him food. He was terribly skinny, which caused me to name him Skinny. He was the outdoor cat that returned every day and spent at least an hour with me before running off. He purred instead of meowed, even when he was hungry. It was the most comforting sound that I could possibly hear.

I went out to call for Skinny, but as I looked around, I saw a hoard of stray cats standing bundled together with their bodies hunched up to attack underneath my uncle's sitting car. They yowled and hissed like an angry mob out for blood. Without thinking, I got on my hands and knees to look closer. Underneath my uncle's car, in the swarm of cats, I spied a tiny black kitten cowering in fear at the incoming attack. Instantaneously, I opted in for his defense, crawling under the rusted car, not caring whether or not I was harmed by teeth, claws, or rusted metal. I was determined to save him. I pushed my way through the mob and took him in my arms. The glaring of cats began to clear until they suddenly vanished, seemingly into thin air. *Had they even been there?*

I crawled out from under the car with one arm pushing me out from the cramped space and the other cradling the bones of the tiny black mass.

Was it even a cat at all? If not, then what was I holding?

I stood up and examined the bundle cradled in my arms. The kitten mewed, showing its teeth.

It looked like a tiny shadow of a black Siberian tiger. From the top to bottom, its teeth were reversed.

He resembled a vampire if his fangs were on the underside, not where canine teeth were found. He also had canine teeth, which were smaller than the underbite fangs that protruded from his tiny face. It was difficult not to notice them once they were seen. I couldn't help but in some way be a little frightened of his appearance, even as I saved him. For this reason, I named him Scary. He must have come off so mean and vicious with those things in his mouth. It was enough reason to burn the witch in the yard.

He was smart since he chose to come here. I lived to save the underdogs. I only saw him for two days until he disappeared. I didn't think much of it, being I had only discovered him before he was attacked. I hope someone took him in as a pet, and he wasn't mauled. I saw no strays for two weeks. Perhaps animal control was called so there were no more strays left. I couldn't offer any of them an actual home anyway. I was barely able to feed them.

Tapping beckoned at the screen door as I was doing my homework. Sitting on the couch, I looked up and discovered dusty fur-lined bones knocking at the door in the shape of a cat. The tapping was followed by a piercing screech, like the sound of nails on a chalkboard, only amplified. The bones were pretending to be a cat.

Its dried vocal cords were unable to form the sound 'meow.' I walked through the door to get a closer look. The colourings matched Skinny's markings, if only he had crawled out of a shallow mud-lined grave and wanted to be fed for his feat. The mud clumped in places of his fur and turned to dust in other areas leaving his off-white fur gray.

He turned his face toward me after I had stood at the door for too long without opening it.

His crystalline eyes glowed goldenrod and bugged out from his eye sockets like a tarsier. When I looked into his eyes, it felt like they were seeing through me.

The feeling made me so dizzy it was challenging to stand. My stomach felt like it was going down an elevator shaft. I stumbled backward, back onto the couch where I had been sitting, cradling my legs in my arms as I stared at the demon possessing Skinny.

Grey had found me and wanted my full attention. He had found a better way to trick me into getting me to get close to him, but I knew by looking into his eyes he was no longer my outside companion, but an imposter.

Why did he keep haunting me? With how much we moved, it was nearly impossible to find me.

Grey stood on his hind legs and began tapping again in hurried confusion. The tapping became a nonstop occurrence. He tried desperately to dig through the glass door.

I begged for the perilous screeching and knocking to stop as I covered my ears with my hands and squinted my eyes shut.

The screeching of the dried vocals of the demon cat must be what it sounds like in hell.

Skinny had never meowed.

Grey had taken over its body, but I was not fooled.

Is this why Grey kept finding me? Because it was unable to trick me? Or was it because I denied it companionship even when it took over the cats I loved? It had been following me since I was a little girl. The cat Jerry left me for was Grey. He just never returned, unlike the others.

At night I laid on the couch and stared at the ceiling, dreading falling asleep. My dreams revolved around the distortion of the cat. The muddy gray mass and the bones protruding from its fur terrorized my dreams.

The cat would smile if he caught me outside alone.

It staggered to me, with each step growing taller, broader, and more human-like until it was fully formed. The mud was gone, and his citron eyes grew three times the size of human eyes.

His paw became hands with daggers for claws. His smile was of the Cheshire cat, only sharper, like a shark.

I asked, "Are you a wolf or a cat?" The shapeshifter turned his head to the side, breathing heavily through his mouth, drooling as it looked me over as my heart beat faster until I woke up. Sometimes he'd be on top of me, punishing my body with his lust.

It growled softly, "I'm not hungry for food." I was helplessly motionless underneath his filth and bones.

There was no doubt in my mind that Skinny was already dead when his body showed up.

I hadn't seen Grey in such a long time that I had almost forgotten all about him, but I knew now that he had never stopped watching me. He didn't desire to be seen until now.

After each nightmare, I felt a sense of deja vu. I never remembered waking up with them before, but it was far too familiar for it to be the first time. Grey could no longer resist his appetites, as he lived on fear, and I was now keeping him full every night. I had underestimated him before.

One night, while I was trying not to sleep, I laid in the dimly lit living room, and the walls began to turn rosy yet dark sepia filtered, containing the atmosphere of both going back in time and aging far into the future. Fines began to grow against the top walls. Trees cracked through the planks of the ceiling. Emptying through as the wood creaked and cracked and collapsed down, losing the battle to the stronger, living wood. It was just as it had been before. I had stopped seeing the house change until now. It happened so slowly, fast compared to how the world works in time, but slow as far as a hallucination works. The Earth was taking back its land before my eyes. The foliage was crumbling down the house as I watched a lifetime within the span of minutes. Skinny jumped down from one of the newly formed branches that intruded the ceiling. His sapphire eyes greeted mine with a purr. He pawed his way up and leaped to the top of the couch. Laying above my feet, he permitted me to sleep, and my dreaming was no more. The transition occurred nightly, with Skinny emerging out of the branches and sleeping above my feet, purring me to sleep like a guardian angel, saving me from the haunting of nightmares and demons. Nothing could harm me as long as he was there. I finally enjoyed sleep, at least until we had to move again.

My uncle's girlfriend kicked us out of the house after another week of staying there, even when Mom paid Andrea the rent she asked for.

Andrea complained as Mom was getting ready for work, "You never do nothing. You're always gone. Leaving these kids expecting me to watch them. Well, I'm done. Get your shit and move out. You were 'posed to be here, taking care of your brother, but you ain't. All you do is take advantage of our charity, and it's about time y'all move on. I'm not raising your kids for you anymore." Andrea would come up with any excuse to irritate Mom, but tonight Mom ended the complaints by setting things in motion to move out that night and skip work.

16. Freedom

I met Mom's boyfriend, Anthony, the day we moved in with him.

Mom and Anthony met smoking meth together, and it seemed she had to have a man to belong to, so why not him?. She had broken up with my Dad months ago, shortly after we moved in with my uncle. Mom had been playing the dating game, but nothing meaningful had worked out on all of her dates until Anthony began to obsess about her.

Anthony was tall and overweight but always seemed to adorn a smile underneath his *Mario*-style mustache. There was nothing spectacular about his appearance, but it led me to the realization that Mom liked obese men with mustaches.

All that mattered was that he seemed to openly adore Mom. He told her that he fell in love with her the first day they met in their mutual group of friends.

Mom hardly felt the same way, even as we moved in with him, but she appreciated being adored. The only things that seemed similar about them were that they both had jobs and smoked meth.

He seemed friendly enough and did more than the other men Mom dated had done before. He gave us a place to stay and made sure we were comfortable. He didn't complain or try to command control.

We lived in a motel again, but the circumstances were better now. Mom shared a room with Anthony, and Orion and I shared the living room. Orion slept on the couch, and I was on the floor for a while until Anthony bought us both an air mattress. Orion had his air mattress in the kitchen, and mine was set up in the living room by the door, so I wouldn't disturb anyone when I snuck in. I was rarely ever home, except to sleep.

I visited the community pool often but often left to enjoy walking around in jeans and a bikini. I was only a few months over 15 but was on the hunt for something exciting.

At first, I caught the attention of a group of teenagers my age that offered to be my friend, but I didn't have much in common with people my age or even teens a couple years older than me. I tried it out for a week, but everyone was plastered to their phones and wanted to talk about what they did on them, or trips to the mall, and how their parents were so mean because they didn't give them what they wanted as soon as they wanted it.

Life is full of small talk and complaints occurring on any average day. I just wanted a sense of adventure, a chase, or simply something I could sink my teeth into. Had I not been on the hunt for something to grab my attention, I might have learned what it felt to be at least somewhat normal.

Normal didn't quite work for me. I didn't want to be enlisted in small talk or walk to nowhere without purpose. Friendship has always felt a bit aloof to me with all the moving around and negative experiences with my peers. Everything was temporary, and if I didn't get enjoyment out of what I was doing or the things happening around me, it hardly seems worth spending time engaging in whatever monotony may be.

When a caged animal is freed, it experiences a period of immobilization from fleeing from its cage. Once it understands freedom again, it runs wild chaotically. An animal born in the wild that has never known captivity understands the dangers of the world and only acts as a savage when in danger because it is the only way to be kept safe from harm. An animal born in an enclosure does not fully grasp the idea of safety, as safety was given in its cage. Safety can be a synonym for imprisonment. Safe does not feel free. It feels like a prison. I was like a caged animal going out into the wild. I understood the concept of danger, but it did not stop me from walking into it. I didn't have to play it safe here. I was a predator in a community of prey, although it could also be seen the other way around. The hunt was mutually encouraged.

Often, what I wanted was yet to be spotted. It wasn't until I did laundry one night around 6 p.m. that I felt the rush of seduction staring at me.

I carried double-stacked baskets of dirty clothes down the stairs of the motel room, three times to the laundry room across the parking lot, loaded the washers with the dirty clothes, started the machines, and began walking back to the motel room. As the warm rush of seduction filled the air, I looked around before revisiting the safety of our suite. I changed my clothes, thinking maybe if I looked a bit more flirty in a black lace mini dress, the eyes I felt would come to me instead of watching like an invisible force.

What if he's old and ugly?

I began laughing at myself. It didn't really matter. It was almost like playing a game with myself. I was entertained even if nobody was watching because of all the euphoria rushing around in my body just from doing the laundry. I went back downstairs to check on the clothes. They only had a few minutes left, so I sat on a counter inside the laundromat, waited until the time was up, and put the clothes in the dryer. I had been sitting idly in the room for ten minutes, and no one came, not even to wash their clothes. I started all six dryers and huffed as I returned to the motel room. I was becoming a bit frustrated, feeling crazy for thinking anyone would be watching me. *It was actually kind of creepy for someone to be watching me every time I went to check the laundry. I needed to change my clothes and not try this strange seduction game.*

I put on a pair of jean shorts and a T-shirt and returned to get them an hour later when the clothes were certain to be dry. I wasn't trying to play games with myself anymore because I felt dumb for wanting someone to watch me and take pleasure from the thought. It was desperate and unattractive.

Three of the dryers were open when I went to get the clothes from the dryer. No clothes were in any washer or dryer, apart from the clothes I had in the dryer.

Why would anyone open the dryers? While I emptied the clothes from the dryer into the laundry baskets, I realized all of my sexy lace g-strings were gone. Why would anyone take them? It must have been a girl. Why would a girl stare at me, thinking I probably had cute panties, and then steal them from the dryer? I couldn't come up with a reasonable answer.

Feeling frustrated about the theft, I loaded the rest of the clothes into the baskets.

A tall man a few years older than me walked in and said, "Hi. Can I help you carry those? It seems like a long way to go by yourself. I'm Ron, by the way."

Ron was a cute stranger with hazel eyes and short curly brown hair. He reminded me a bit of Drew, apart from the curls. His eyes were hazel, and he was quite fetching, so what was the harm?

I replied, "Sure, if you want. Do you know anything about missing panties?"

He blushed, "I can't say I do. I've been watching you for a minute. I didn't see anyone else here. Do you mind if I ask... Why do you keep changing your clothes?"

It was my turn to blush.

Instead of responding, I picked up a double load of baskets and walked back to the motel room. He followed behind me, carrying two as well, until we dropped them off and returned for the last two. When we were finished, he asked if I wanted to look out at the stars with him.

We sat on the stairs outside of the motel room I called home and talked about the constellations, zodiac signs, and psychology.

He was interesting, deep, and humorous, and by the end of the night, I discovered the pleasure I could receive from being bitten on my neck. It transformed pain into pleasure. I had never been bitten like that before. As the pleasure continues, my body pulsed in desire from wanting to feel his inside me.

I snuck into our suite with him and felt his sensual hands

all over my body, biting and kissing in chaotic turns until I could think of nothing more than the heat between my thighs burning for him. For some reason, as he entered me, I thought of telling him to stop, but I didn't.

I wanted him, but part of me didn't want his sex inside of me once it was about to happen. I couldn't say why, as overcome with desire as I was.

The night ended strangely when he left right after he came, claiming he was running late to get home. *He hadn't been in a hurry the rest of the time*

I didn't see him for a couple of days after we had sex. I was beginning to give up on him until he called me and invited me to his suite. We had sex again on his grandmother's bed that he lived with, as someone else was in his room. He invited me to his room after we were done and introduced me to his boyfriend. I suddenly felt betrayed, although I tried to seem accepting.

I broke up with him a few days afterward. I wasn't into sharing my time with another person or being treated like a second choice.

I found a replacement for Ron a couple of days afterward when I saw the sexiest guy in the entire complex, maybe the entire city. I chanced upon walking by on the pavement of the walkway outside. He was going to visit a friend, but I was lucky enough to catch him on his way out. He was hypnotizing. His eyes were the lightest shade of brown, almost making them colorless. His soft black hair bounced gently as he walked. I was almost jealous of his hair, being able to bounce on him so nonchalantly out in the open all the time. His skin was dark and light at the same time, pale yet rich, tan but natural. I tried to walk by him casually as I walked past him on the stairwell, but I couldn't help the fire in my loins from burning all the way through me as we passed one another. I couldn't help but look behind me afterwards. When I did, I caught him, his neck already turned, staring at my butt. The butterflies exploded in my stomach in hyperactive glee. *Was **this guy** checking **me** out?*

I turned fully in his direction and bit my lip, and I

exclaimed, "God damn, you're sexy... Fuck!" He smiled brightly as he turned to come back up the stairs he had just walked down. As he walked towards me, my knees felt weak, my ankles barely capable of sustaining my weight. I felt like I was going to faint as dots encompassed my vision, and it began to tunnel. I tried to shake the feeling off as the sexy stranger reached me and held out his hand.

He smiled confidently as he said, "Hello, hotness. I'm Aaron. What may I call you, beautiful?"

I stammered, "Anytime you want... Anything you want. I mean... Hi, I'm Storm."

I gave him the number for the motel room, and he often called me at night, strumming his guitar and singing my favorite song, *Outside by Staind.*

Unfortunately, he had a girlfriend at the motel complex. Hence, all we had together were our occasional late-night talks and secret obsessions with one another that would occasionally turn into a lustful hour of ripping off one another's clothes, but that didn't happen very often. Most of the time, I only saw him hanging out with his girlfriend or in his Jeep.

Random men would show up in our motel room, visiting my mom to buy or sell dope from her. . Sometimes, they would look at me like I was a piece of meat they wanted to devour. I was rarely interested in any of them, except for two I began trying to seduce.

I knew where one of them lived, a guy who went by Shorty, so one day, I unexpectedly showed up at his door. Shorty never looked at me like he wanted to eat me, but I could feel the chemistry anytime I was in any room with him. He wasn't extraordinarily handsome, but he made up for it with his confidence and brightly colored eyes. He was short but had enough of a swagger about him to make up for whatever he lacked.

When he answered his door, I whispered, "I've been working on a dance routine, but I haven't had anywhere to practice. Would you mind telling me if I'm getting better at dancing, or at least let me practice with you? It would mean the world to me."

Shorty invited me in and brought a dining room chair into the middle of the living room.

Did he know what I meant when I asked him to watch me dance?

I tried to be as sexy as possible while I performed my first tease of a lap dance, slowly rocking my hips every second to hypnotize him with my body until the song he played was through. It went exactly the way I had wanted it to go.

Once my dance ended, he coughed, "Wow. I didn't know it was going to be like that."

I giggled, "I did."

He grabbed me by my hips, causing me to straddle his lap.

He smiled as he tried to think of how he wanted to word what he wanted to say as I softly pulsed by the body against his. He asked, "Did you come here planning on doing that when you came over?"

I breathed on his neck, dragging my lips across his flesh, whispering, "Yeah, why not? Am I such a bad girl? Do you want to punish me for coming over to seduce you?"

He stammered, "No… you're good. You're…fuck, you're so bad. Yes, I'm going to punish that pussy. Anytime you want, just tell me your pussy is hungry, and I got you."

We started kissing while I straddled him in the chair until he carried me to his bedroom and gently threw me on his bed. He showed me what good sex is, and how freeing the act can be when you let the animal inside out. The savagery was nothing short of art.

I had a weekly habit of knocking on his door until he found a girlfriend and tried to pawn me off on his brother when I came over early in the morning when I couldn't sleep.

Shorty claimed he had to go into town for something and would return soon, but that wasn't true. He told his twin brother to seduce me because sex was what I wanted when I came over.

Initially, I sat on the couch next to him, waiting for

Shorty to come back until he began to touch me. I laughed as I declined his efforts, but he pulled my baggy jeans down from my hips to show the black lace boy shorts I had on underneath. He claimed those panties were his kryptonite, along with my flat stomach.

It set off his hunting instinct, so it was a chase around Shorty's motel room until I escaped through the front door.

Shorty wanted to be loyal to his new girlfriend. Shorty was setting me up with his twin, so theoretically, transferring my desire over should've been simple, except they were definitely not the same person. The chemistry was nonexistent. I didn't have a type exactly, but the most attractive thing about Shorty was his charisma. I could tell whenever he was near because the back of my neck got hot, and my skin tingled softly. It was why I wanted him. I only felt desperation from his brother, which had no appeal to me.

Aaron called me for the first time in weeks and said, "Hey, long time no talk. I need to ask you a question. It's about Ron."

I said, "Okay."

He sighed, "I've been given some information, and since you knew him well, I just wanted to get your opinion."

I occasionally hung out with Ron for short periods until he found a new girlfriend named Sheila. She looked surprisingly a lot like me, with white blonde hair and green eyes, with only a smaller forehead and perhaps even a year or two younger. She looked like a sweet girl. Sheila walked around in a baggy black T-shirt and had a friend walking next to her named Trina. Sheila was new to the complex and, from what I understood, had recently broken up with Ron.

Trina yelled, "Hey, you know what that piece of shit AIDs-ridden motherfucker did to this girl?"

I asked, "Who?"

Trina gruffed, "Ron. Both your ex-boyfriends. Girl, tell her what you told me."

Sheila spoke softly, "Well, I had slept with him before, but one night I had invited him inside, and he was on top of me in bed, and he raped me."

I asked, confused, "What?"

Trina exclaimed, "Yeah, he raped her, and now she's pregnant with a rape baby! How fucked up is that? It probably has AIDS too and she has to give birth to that! Her uterus is going to fall out and rot and it's all his fault!"

I asked again, "What?... How? When? How far along are you?"

Sheila elaborated, "Well, Ron and I were dating, and we'd had sex before, but one night, he came in and lay in bed with me until he got on top of me and raped me. It was a couple weeks ago, so I'm that far along. I'm not showing yet, but I wear baggy clothes, so my parents won't know when it begins to show. I just don't know what to do about it."

I said, "Wow. I'm so sorry. Did you tell him to stop or scream for help? How did your parents not hear?"

She cleared her throat and stammered, "Well, I never said anything. I didn't tell him to stop or not to. I just didn't really want to do it."

I nodded my head and said, "I see."

Trina barked, "Yeah, That's why I walk with her, to make sure nothing bad happens to her again."

I repeated, "I see. Good luck to you both. I'm sorry that you feel that way. Just one more question, if you never said no, then how was it rape?"

Sheila cleared her throat, "Well, I guess it wasn't, but it kind of was."

Trina began to rush away with Sheila, saying, "We've gotta go. Here he comes now. We're not getting raped again, no way."

I stayed where I stood to talk to Ron to get his story for the sake of curiosity.

"...Yeah, she says she's pregnant, and I don't know what to do. I'm not even allowed to talk to her. She won't let me," Ron said.

I thought for a moment and replied, "I don't think anyone can know if they're pregnant for sure in that short of time. It's only been a couple weeks, right?

He looked down as he stammered, "Well...yeah."

I smiled at him as I said, "I'm sorry for what she's saying about you. She never said no or stop, right? So it wasn't rape. I'll vouch for you if anyone asks."

He smiled back jubilantly as he said, "Thank you. Thank you so much. You have no idea how much that means. I will probably need you to. She's trying to get someone to come to beat my ass, and that's the other reason I don't know what to do. Can I hug you?"

I hugged him, and we went our separate ways.

That's what led to this phone call. Aaron's girlfriend was Trina's sister. He didn't look much like a fighter, but he knew many people who would for the right price.

I told Aaron my story and how Ron was almost in tears about it the last time I spoke to him.

Aaron asked, "So why does everyone keep saying he has AIDS?

I sighed, knowing why, but disliking the answer, "It's because of his boyfriend. He's had the same boyfriend for years. I met him once. Trina thinks everyone that's gay has AIDS."

He inhaled sharply, "I see. Yeah, that's bullshit. I know who you're talking about, and he's clean if that's the reason why.. Thank you for all of this. Maybe I'll come by later this week to come see you."

Part of me felt excited, but the other part of me spoke instead, "That's alright. You seem pretty happy with your girlfriend. I'm not trying to get in the way of that."

He whispered, "I wish I met you before I got with her... I'm sorry I didn't tell you when we met. I just... I don't know what I was doing."

I smiled as I spoke, "That's okay. I would've been more than thrilled to be yours, but I get it. She's really pretty."

Mom and Anthony were off somewhere when Orion and I heard a knock at the door. I ignored the banging without seeing who was at the door, but after a few minutes, the door opened unexpectedly, and a skinny old woman with gray ragged hair walked in as if she belonged in our motel room. She was talking on her cell phone as she walked in with a woman I had seen before.

She screeched at the phone, "I'm at the home wrecker's trash den now with her two little ugly brats. I'm going to hang her by her neck from the chandelier. She has no idea who she's messing around with. No good harlot ought to have her car and her face smashed in. I'll be the one to do it for her, messin' with a married man, breaking up a happy marriage. Dirty homewrecking whore."

I kept interrupting her, yelling, "Who are you?! I don't know you! Get out!"

The more it became obvious that she was talking about Mom, the louder I became until she reached where I stood by Mom's door.

I growled one last time, "Get the fuck out before I make you leave. I don't know who you are, and you've trespassed too far now."

Orion sat on the back of the couch, watching fearfully.

She snickered, "What are you going to do about it, little girl?"

The warnings are over now.

I began pushing the intruder with full force repeatedly until she was back outside on the pavement stairwell. I thought about pushing her over the railing, but I turned around instead as I did what I needed to do by removing her from our home.

I stepped towards the motel room to leave her outside the door, but my hair was wrapped in her grasp. I was taken by surprise and pulled back in front of her.

I began to yell, "I'm fifteen! I'm underage! You better let go... You better fucking not..."

I was met with her claws ravaging my face and body. Her talons tore at my clothes, pulling the white Ambercrombie tube top I had on, revealing my bare chest.

She was trying to take my clothes off! What the hell! What kind of fight was this?

I struggled to keep my breasts from being exposed as I tried to defend myself.

I managed to trip her down on the pavement and grabbed her face in my hands and tried to gouge her eyes out with my thumbs. The woman she came with pulled me off of her, yelling at me to stop. I wasn't trying to fight. I only wanted to stop being clawed and topless.

As soon as she stood up, the clawing continued. Blood dripped down my face onto my arm. My shirt was being pulled off again. I stopped to pull my shirt back down where it needed to be. I was beyond aggravated. Our fight was only pulled apart if I was winning. I couldn't do anything to get away from her claws.

I yelled, "Stop! Leave my fucking clothes alone. I'm fifteen. You're assaulting a minor!"

She brought a friend with her that was on the phone with the police, claiming I attacked her. With my hair in her hand, I pushed her to the ground, pulling me down with her.

A couple came down their stairs to walk their dog and broke up the attack.

The woman tried to relate, "I used to get in fights with my mom like this all the time."

I said, "Umm.. okay."

I looked back at the intruder and shouted, "I'm calling 911. You need to leave." The woman sneered, "I already got them on the phone bitch. They're taking you to jail. You and your dope fiend mother."

I called the police, and they informed me that they were already on their way.

I waited outside the door for the cops to come.

The stranger with her dog asked, "Is... this not your mom?"

I coughed, "No! I don't know that woman. She just came strolling into my house, so I pushed her out, and then she attacked me and kept trying to rip my clothes off."

The neighbor turned pale as she uttered, "Oh. I'll stay with you until the police come, if you want. Where's your mom?"

I replied, "I don't know. Just gone, I guess."

Three officers stomped up the stairs and asked the old woman to go downstairs with them. One of the officers stayed to take my statement. I told them what happened, and my face and hands were photographed many times to capture every scratch and drop of blood. I had a deep gash going down the right side of my face, from my forehead to my lips. The officer comforted, "She's going to go to jail for a long time for this."

Mom and Anthony walked up the stairs, confused about what was happening.

Mom looked at my face and exclaimed, "Storm! What happened to your face?"

I yelled, "That bitch down there did it. I just wanted her to leave our room, so I pushed her, and she did this to me!"

The old woman yelled something in return that I couldn't decipher.

The police spoke to one another to compare statements.

Orion had opened the door for them, which was how they came in. The old woman was Anthony's ex-wife, who somehow found out where we lived. The woman was handcuffed and sitting at the bottom of the stairs until Anthony took one of the officers to the side and whispered in their ear.

The cops whispered to one another with confused expressions. Instantly, she was released from their custody, and everyone began to walk away, shaking their heads.

My mom yelled, "What did you say?! No, don't leave. She needs to go to jail for what she's done to my daughter."

Anthony scooted her inside, and I followed. He never told either of us what he said that swept it all under the rug.

It caused such a detrimental issue that Anthony left for two months without telling anyone where he was going or why. Without Anthony there to support us, Mom had to find a job again. She had quit working at the strip club after a few weeks of being with Anthony. Rent was coming up, so Mom began working as an escort. She even found an actor to be her hobbyist. She only really needed one guy to help pay the rent at the motel, although another man began showing up as her dope dealer, he once asked me if I do what my mom does, and if so, he'd pay. Maybe if he was cute, I would've seen the appeal, but everything about him felt dirty.

It was probably for the best for me to think Mom only had one guy to date for money. I didn't see anything wrong with it. Honestly, I thought that's what she would do anyway with her way of getting over men. She was just being paid for it, so she was making the most of what she enjoyed.

If you do what you love, you'll never work a day in your life.

Anthony returned home and acted as if he had never left.

The first question he asked was, "Did you sleep with anyone while I was away?"

Mom lied, "No, did you?"

He also lied and said no. After seeing his ex-wife, Anthony returned to her for the entirety of his time away.

His second question was what she did to pay the rent for the motel, seeing she didn't have a job. She said she did some odd jobs here and there. He never said what he did with his time away or why he had left.

If you never admit your wrongdoings, you never have to lie. Or if you always lie, you never have to admit what you did wrong.

Anthony received a job offer that couldn't be refused, so we moved into a three-bedroom apartment in Oklahoma. It was the nicest apartment that I had ever seen. All of the rooms were massive. I started ninth grade late, in October. The school was a massive three-story building with more people than I cared to think about. Mom let me dye my hair bright pink to get me to go to school because I had thought I didn't have to go back since everyone else had started school two months ago. Mom dropped out in eighth grade, so why couldn't I?

I met with my school counselor, that stated my time may not count since I was beginning ninth grade late. She told me I could go with the normal learning plan as everyone else, or I could pick random things I liked since I may not be credited. I decided to go to random classes that sounded interesting.

I enjoyed Debate class. I started off very shy because I've never enjoyed speaking. I did well on paper and typically declined any speaking roles until I was chosen by the class to debate on the topic of public domain. I had difficulty looking straight forward instead of at the other girl debating the opposite point of the matter with me. She wasn't as knowledgeable about the study materials we were given before starting the debate, so I won by a landslide. It was fun being applauded after winning. It wasn't so bad after all. I have constantly been programmed to feel like less than anything positive, smart, or worthy of praise. I still didn't like talking in front of a crowd.

Criminal justice was more of how I thought Debate would be. Our assignment each day was to pick a story from a newspaper and talk about it with the class, often yelling across the room in no specific order. I mostly slept through this class because I didn't want to socialize or argue across the room with everyone as the rest of the class did. It was too loud. I accepted failure easily.

Zoology, which I thought would be exciting, was more of a study of bacteria, less interesting than biology, and had seemingly nothing to do with animals. It was unfortunate because I really wanted to be allowed to touch the animals in the zoo, and to make a living that way would be an unfathomable dream. I had no idea how zookeepers get that job, so it seemed unlikely I would ever get to have that experience. I stopped paying attention in this class as well.

I was also failing algebra because I came in the middle of an assignment and had no idea of even the basic algebra formulas. Sometimes my guesswork gave me an A; other times, it gave me a more expected grade of C or F. The logical part of it was give-and-take. If it made sense without knowing the formula that had been learned before I started school, I did well. Otherwise, it was gibberish, and I didn't know where numbers and letters were supposed to go or when.

Art was enjoyable, since I thought of myself as an artist. I often drew in my free time in and out of school. The only other class I enjoyed was Aerobics, which started roughly when we were first told to run laps for thirty minutes at a time. I lost my breath often, needing to slow down and walk until my heart rate and breath returned to normal, but the more I ran, the more I enjoyed it.

I hadn't made any friends and was on the verge of giving up entirely.

Anthony asked me to go check the mail after I got home from school.

I got lost along the way.

17. Walking Nightmare

I could always tell my dreams from reality, despite the nightmarish things I saw in both. The only way I knew the difference was by location. Obviously, it wasn't a foolproof method.

What we dream, be it wonderful or terrifying, holds a deeper meaning other than what initially comes to mind. It's hypothesized that dreams may be a way to process trauma and show you what you need from life as well as from yourself. Your brain holds a filing cabinet of ideas, memories, and desires. Acceptance is the only way to get rid of something haunting your mind and be able to move on.

It often took time to decipher my dreams. It's often difficult to recover from the horrors of a nightmare and be able to pull out the inner meaning from a neutral point of view.

A recurring nightmare I had took place at my grandparent's trailer home. Walking into their home, nothing was out of the ordinary. Even the sliding glass door was equally as difficult for me to open as it was in real life. Dust covered the floor, only slightly more than usual, making the floor look browner than it actually was. I walked around calling out for Granny and Papa until I entered the only place besides the back room I hadn't been, their bedroom. A noise or sudden movement would catch my attention. If it were a movement, it was the sudden appearance of long, black, interconnected snakes all around. There were so many slithering black bodies there was no room to walk. The snakes hung from the ceiling and swarmed Papa's bed.

If it were a sound that distracted me from looking for my grandparents, it was the noise of the cracking ceiling that was bound to collapse at any moment from the weight of the snakes coiling above. There was no escape after the newly formed slithering river finished pouring down. As long as I remained in my grandparent's room, as much as the snakes frightened me, they would never cause me any harm. It was the running that did me in, the false sense of safety at any point once I thought I got away.

Sometimes I'd run into the bathroom across their room to escape, even when I had no plan for a way out, just to hide from the snakes overtaking Papa's room. Only, it wasn't safe. More bodies hung from the shower ceiling and were embedded within the shower walls. They even slithered up from inside the toilet and tried to bite. More would spring from closed cabinet doors and darkened corners.

I never dared to go into the back room. That room has always been creepy, perhaps even haunted. I'm sure it was filled to the brim with snakes, but maybe if I ever looked in that room, a gaping pink mouth wouldn't hit me right in the face when I tried to escape through the glass door. Once I was bitten, I would wake up feeling as if I had been swallowed whole.

In my depiction, the snakes seemed to signify secrets. Untold truths that, if ever said out loud, would cause such an uproar, it would be like setting loose a house full of snakes. It would have been a mystery as to what the dream meant had Mom never told me about my papa. She only told me because I saw a wonderful, caring, and loving man; she saw something within him that was much different. He was her source of shame, why she chose poorly with men, and why she had an all-encompassing desire to run away from everything, even if it only led her to another trap. I'm sure there were more secrets slithering through my grandparents' house. I had briefly been told more stories about my aunt and uncles, consisting of tales of incest and abuse of one another. The only thing was that since Mom was the storyteller I was never given such a depiction of her own misdeeds.

I'm not sure whose secrets were decimating the house with snakes, but someone was definitely hiding more than they could bear. Even if I knew what they were, I wouldn't go around telling everyone, or perhaps even anyone. I liked it when secrets remained with me. It led me to a growing curiosity I didn't know how to absolve.

Sometimes you can have a psychokinetic power that allows what other people think or feel to get conjured within your mind. Some call these psychic powers, but it's never been when I wanted it to happen. I couldn't control what or when my gift would occur. It just appears in my mind sometimes, more often in dreams than any other medium.

I imagined it was on Papa's mind, how he hoped I would never find out. How would I ever look at him the same for the way that he was instead of the man he had shown me my entire life? I'm sure it felt heavy carrying that secret around. Or was someone else thinking of all the secrets slithered around that house? It could've been Mom replaying old unwanted memories that she couldn't say out loud. Who was never certain and unable to be answered at any time.

I used to dream of Granny drowning quite

frequently. I watched so closely I could feel the air in her lungs running out, as her body struggled to get free from the water's grasp. Nothing ever held her down aside from the water itself. She never learned how to swim and was terrified of drowning. Perhaps I was having a nightmare for her or joining in one she could be having simultaneously. Or maybe it was how she felt being awake all the time and living with unending resentment.

What else reoccurred?...

I screamed for a time, but my mouth was covered until I whispered, "no."

Tears streamed down my body, smearing against the naked shadow and myself. His thrust never altered, regardless of how I cried or tried to physically stop him. Physical aggression only caused a hand to cover my mouth or my face to be palmed, making me feel even more powerless. His body moved in the motion of sickening waves pulsating into my unwilling body. I never fought back, not truly. I didn't do the heroic, self-preserving thing where you bite, claw, punch, and kick in order to get away and defend yourself. I was too afraid.

I was forced into empty rooms and thrown onto the floor. The shadow climbed on top of me repeatedly, always wanting more. My tears were like adrenaline to his sex. I was taken back to his car and yearned to go home, but I was only taken further away. I was his prize he yearned to show off. Another location, another friend of his inviting us in as I whimpered, "save me."

The response given at any time was not what I wanted to hear, a muttering voice repeated, "I don't need this shit."

Another hour went by with another drive, another place, just for it to happen again.

How do I make it stop? How do I find a way home?

The answer came when I walked out to a mob that had formed outside an upstairs apartment I was last taken to. I had been dragged everywhere I had been taken up until now. The shadow had his hand gripped around my arm, holding me by the railing, leaving me unable to move.

Angry faces screamed, "You don't belong here!", "Yeah!", "This ain't yo hood, white girl!".

Glass bottles were held in hands of the people shouting, ready to be thrown.

How did so many people gather around so quickly? Why were they even awake?

They had been preparing as I was being raped inside. They didn't know or care why I was there. They just didn't like that I was on their side of the street. The shadow pressed me harder against the railing, ready for the mob to attack and give me up as a sacrifice. Two bottles were thrown, hitting the stairs, but missing me. They exploded at the railing by my bare feet. More bottles were raised in hands, and someone even lit one on fire with a rag coming out from its vase. The attack ceased before it got ugly when one gentleman stepped out from his apartment across the way.

He came out of his home wearing a red and white letter jacket, speaking firmly, *"We don't do this here. This is a person. She is alive."*

The crowd argued but began to back up and talk among one another.

"Let her pass," the man with the letter jacket said. He was the only good man I saw that night. He saved me from being a blood sacrifice. I was pushed past him as I stumbled down the steps and back into the green abyss, saved from a mob but not from the shadow.

I was finally taken home as the sun began to rise. I stumbled quickly up the stairs to my apartment, sick from being alive. I walked into the dark apartment that was home, stumbling through the hallway, and turned on the bathroom light. I sat in the shower, disgusted by the sight of my own body, unable to do anything but horrendously cry.

Turning on the water was more difficult than walking. Imagining being clean felt unnatural. uncomfortable, like an impossible feat.

What should I do? What could I possibly tell anyone? I would not tell anyone anything. Nobody would say anything then. Punish me for being out all night. That's fine. I deserve it. I found the rebel smile, a sense of relief, in only ever having to confess what had been done to me, to myself. Nobody had to know. It never happened. It wasn't real. I imagine things; it's what I do.

I stood up from the tub and turned the water on to make the evidence on my body wash away like the water down the drain. I scrubbed until all the marks were my own inflictions of being scathed from scrubbing, burned from the heat of the water, and scraped by the pull of the soap brush against my blistering skin.
I did this to myself, nothing more.

I washed inside my vagina to cleanse the slime flowing out of it. I was tired of the fear I felt. I was exhausted from living within my skin. I grabbed a towel and faded into my room, pressing it into my skin and brushing it off as harshly as possible. My face was puffy from the tears that night, feeling more like a corpse than a living body. It was just a bad dream.

The first time I woke up to the horror, my entire body hurt. My skin was missing a layer, and bruises were all over me. I hid a black eye for several days, convincing myself I must have punched myself in my sleep. I must have tried to itch my skin off, it had to have been an allergic reaction to something that had been ingested that night. Maybe there were ants on the floor that bit me all over. I had poison ivy somehow.

Whatever anyone wished to think, that's exactly what happened. Nobody thought I had been gone that night. I must not have been. I just fell asleep early. I fell asleep before I went to check the mail. I forgot, I didn't get lost. I never went out. I hadn't been taken. No. It was just a bad dream. My mind made it up. That's all that happened. Some details changed sometimes. Sometimes he took me from my stairwell, pulled me in his car, drove across the complex parking lot, got on top of me, and took me back. It wasn't as bad as the first time. He just came back for more. Another time he knocked on the door, and Mom answered. When I came to the door, he tapped his gun across his leg and told me to go with him if I knew what was good for me. I had to go to keep my family safe.

The nightmare occurred more than twice a week, up to every night if I was unpropitious enough.
What was the meaning of it, of the dream?

...It meant that I was in denial.

18. Undeniable

Mom's go-to after any breakup was my father. We had not seen him since he was taken to jail. It seemed at least she was out of love with him this time. She only needed him to cure her chemical dependency, as Oklahoma didn't seem to have any meth.

Dad and I never reconnected after he broke my trust before. I was fatherless, as far as I could tell. He was just a sperm donor that kept coming back for more.

To be fair, we couldn't connect because he saw me as a whore. I was a pregnant fifteen-year-old that claimed her pregnancy was rape. I withheld what had been done to me until Mom took me to the doctor for the incessant itch of my skin. She thought I might have scabies, and the doctor should be able to get rid of the parasite crawling underneath my skin. We left the doctor's office with a battle of anti-itch medication, as nothing seemed to cause the reaction, and given the information that I was two months pregnant after a test had been done. I would have said nothing had it not been for this series of events.

Dad feared I would give my unborn child to his parents to adopt, as his sister had done when she was too young to raise a child herself.

Nobody really thought that I had been raped. It was an excuse that I used to somehow make my unplanned pregnancy acceptable.

Strangely, my one advocate was Dad's meth dealer. He woke up from a nightmare and scribbled on a sheet of paper by his bed that I had been raped. He called Mom to tell him a week after it had happened, but with no one knowing, it seemed like he just had a bad dream. He also showed my father the note he had written when he saw him on one of his trips back to Texas. Their dealer thought it was so important that he kept it. He told him to believe me, which of course, to Dad, was bullshit.

How could they know I tried to come up with anything I could to make him not want me. I told him that I was a virgin (*which only made him want me more*), that I was only fifteen (*he didn't care*), and that I had AIDS (*"Lemme find out"*). I cried and told him to just take me home, but I didn't get to go home until he was done thoroughly.

Strangers asked questions every day, even people that might've been called friends otherwise. "Why weren't you hurt?", "Why didn't he kill you?", or "Why did you not fight back if you didn't want it?"

Why should I have to? Why should I be questioned? Why does it even matter?

I have always been paralyzed with fear, and this was not any different. I was only worried about being left somewhere, being shot, and having my family killed if I didn't allow what he wanted to occur. I knew he had a gun he kept under the hood of his green Ford Taurus. He brought it with him sometimes. If he knew how or when to use it, I couldn't be certain, but I didn't want to take my chances. My flight or fight response is neither, but to freeze.

Nobody should have to die because someone thought I was pretty. I shouldn't have to die just to protect my own body. How I felt should've been enough to let me say that I had been raped, but if there's no evidence, it didn't happen. I wasn't trying to press charges. I didn't want to be condemned as a whore by everyone, especially my family. All I wanted to do was wash it away, just like I had tried that morning of the event, scrub the feeling away, inside and out. But I couldn't, as his seed had stuck, and I was carrying the only evidence that didn't classify as proof.

"I bet the baby comes out white," as my father would say.

When a white girl gets pregnant by a black man, it's often claimed as rape. I didn't want to be another statistic, giving a reason to deserve to be attacked by a mob, true or false. There are too many hate crimes going on in the world, the way I see it. Too many innocent men sit in jail because someone lied about being raped. Nobody thinks anyone tells the truth about it unless the semen is caught slipping out and tested right after it occurs. Going to a hospital right after the event instead of trying to wash it away. It takes bravery and honestly, I wasn't strong enough to do. I just wanted it to go away, and that was no longer possible. I never thought it would come to this. Why would your body choose to keep something no part of you wants? Babies were supposed to be made out of love, not this.

Mom took me to an abortion clinic in town the next week. I was given a sonogram to check the embryo's size, listen to its heart, and be certain of how far along the pregnancy was. I was two months pregnant, as the pregnancy test had said.

The baby had a strong heartbeat and was growing as it should. The bill to abort would be four thousand dollars, and the rate would increase by two hundred dollars weekly. After watching the sonogram, we waited for the doctor in an empty exam room.

Mom promised, "I'll work so hard. So much harder than I already am. I'll work all the shifts if this is what you really want. Just tell me, and I will."

I thought about it, looking at her and then up at the ceiling. I was trying to ask my star what I should do. *What can I do? It was too much. What's done is done.*

I looked back at Mom and replied, "No. It's alright. It's too much. I don't want you to do that to yourself again. You'll get lost."

Mom nodded sorrowfully and then smiled, "Would you maybe want to adopt? …Or do you want to keep it?"

I replied, "No, definitely, I don't want to keep it. But adoption would be better anyways. Nothing should have to die for me."

My father returned every weekend to be with Mom. He carried chemicals across the border for her, as that's what she actually needed him for. She worked long hours waitressing, as she did when he stopped working as a truck driver. She needed to be awake to make the money as long as her body would allow. It was easier with the substance. She never asked him to stay, only to come back with more dope, until the night she told him to never return.

I woke up from my bed of blankets on the living room floor to the worst fight they ever had.

Objects crashed behind the closed door, and Mom screamed, "Get out!"

Dad spat back, "You're nothing but a dope whore! Fuck this!"

I got up and grabbed a butcher knife from the kitchen. It sounded like the walls were crashing down in

Mom's room. It was difficult not to rush in, but I sat still instead of moving.

I waited as I sat on my bed on the floor. If she died, it would give me amnesty for his murder. I would have the upper hand sitting there beside the door, ready to spring up and attack. I could do this. I was ready. With each loud sound, my adrenaline increased, determined to end Dad's life.

Mom's bedroom door burst open as Dad stormed out. He stopped by my feet and turned to say something, but the words never slipped out.

Mom was covered in bruises and blood as she crawled through the door, spewing blood out of her mouth. I only saw her because the light was on in her room.

The chaos had gone on long enough. I stood up and punched the knife into his chest as hard as possible. My hand was stuck holding the knife, afraid of myself and surprised by my own actions. It was done before I knew it like the knife had burst from my hands and taken me with it.

Adrenaline gave Mom the ability to stand up as she saw me freeze. She limped over and opened the front door. I pulled the knife out of his chest and pushed him out. He went plummeting down the stairs outside of the apartment.

Mom slammed the door in the midst of me watching him fall down the stairs and fall short of hitting the bottom. She locked the door in front of us. Never had a locked door felt so safe.

If he lived, I'd never know. Mom turned around and stumbled, so I put her arm around the back of my neck and helped her back to bed. I slept peacefully that night beside her, like I had when I was a baby. Murder occurring out of love has a way of bonding two people that have been lost to one another back together. I'm not sure where we had gotten so lost before, why she had stopped loving me the way she did when I was a toddler. But that love seemed like it was shining through. It made it worth everything I had ever been through. If I had gone to jail even, it would've been worth it because I avenged Mom's life and got back love. It's all I had ever wanted.

Her disbelief in me faded away as we created a new bond, and was replaced with pride.

She took me to my first concert when I was six months pregnant. Nobody thought we were mother and daughter but assumed that we were lovers instead. Nobody that night looked at me like a whore.

It would've been the best day of my life had an old woman not kept her elbow in my stomach for two hours as Mom and I tried to get to the front row to get closer to the band, Staind, that we came to see. As Staind came on stage, everything around me began to blur into black nothingness. I grew increasingly dizzy, too nauseated to stand. I was on the verge of vomiting and tried to ignore my body's distress. All I wanted was to see Staind with her. It was my favorite band, my reward, my gift of Mom's love. It was everything I wanted, but I couldn't enjoy it as I began to unwillingly lean, trying not to faint as the woman's elbow was damaging the baby's entire environment. I lasted as long as I could.

Mom walked me to the bathroom in the back to drench my face in faucet water, drinking it from my hands as I tried to regain my ability to breathe.

19. Choosing Birth

I dropped out of school a few weeks after my pregnancy test. I was sleeping constantly and failing classes entirely because I wouldn't wake up in time for school or slept through the classes instead of learning. Being awake before noon was a task all on its own. Instead, I kept the apartment clean and tried to look into adoption agencies. However, that was difficult since the only phone that I had to use was the payphone outside the apartment complex, and my only way to access the internet was when Mom took me to the library.

Every moment I stepped outside, I was thrown into a state of paranoia, searching for shadows following me, expecting my rapist to find me. Everyone who had ever violated me has walked free, which was no different than now.

If you want justice, you have to create your own. *Darkness overtakes this world. Anything not one with it takes a chance just to exist among the endless shadows. The innocent, the blind, and those that have never known anything but kindness are lucky. Somehow I have always known, even as a child. Maybe it was because I was one of the shadows, or maybe I was not born with such luck.*

My only hope was to avoid the shadow and find my unborn child a home where he would be safe and wanted. I felt like I was carrying a child meant for them, whoever they were.

I thought the gay community might be the most opportune place for him to thrive. Gay marriage at the time of his development was still prohibited. Single adoption was frowned upon, but for a homosexual to adopt a child was blasphemy.

I ignored agencies for this reason when considering adoption options, so Mom took me to the library often to find happy individuals that wanted to adopt online. I wrote down their phone numbers and names to call when it was almost time to give birth to tell them they had a baby on the way.

I had one couple in mind, which included an African American man and a Caucasian man, as my baby would be both. It would be like they had him together, especially since he couldn't be conceived by them alone.

What I didn't consider were the politics of the baby's conception.

Nurture vs. Nature.

*How can a child **not** be born innocent? How can one become like the parents that they have never known? I didn't understand this at the time. I hadn't even thought of it because it was beyond my comprehension.*

Is there a rapist gene in DNA? Is there a poor gene spliced between cells?

Abortion is cursed as murder, save the babies, right? But what do you do with a criminal embryo? I wasn't aware there was such a thing, but trying to have my fetus adopted proved that many people think so.

*Would **you** want a child born out of rape?*

Some answering this question may find an answer they didn't expect. I certainly did not see the outcome, as I thought I had already found the parents of my unborn baby.

When we moved back to Texas to a motel with Mom's ex-boyfriend, Tony, I called the couple. I finally had a phone I could call from indoors.

The phone rang, and a kind voice answered. I suddenly became nervous. My palms were sweating so much that it was difficult to keep the phone receiver from slipping out of my hand. I cleared my throat and took a deep breath.

I tried to sound warm when I said, "Hello, is this Chance?"

He replied, "Well, yes, it is. Hello. May I ask who this is?"

I felt increasingly anxious as I began to stutter, "I saw your adoption port..portfolio, profile online after I was looking for a couple to adopt my baby. My unborn baby, that's.. He's seven months along now. I just... I haven't had a phone, but I saved your number from the computer and have been waiting to call. But I just, I liked you since I read what you had written. I just wanted to know if you still wanted to adopt? If you haven't already found someone else. He's.. he'll be black and white just like you and your boyfriend, so it made you guys that much more perfect to be his fathers. I just want him to be loved, and I think you'd be the best family to do it."

He took an excited inhale until he breathed out, and his voice went a little deeper, showing worry as he asked, "So, why don't you want the baby yourself? How did his conception occur?"

These were the make-or-break questions that led to

being denied as I told him I was only fifteen and not ready to have a child and was worried, even if I wanted to, that I would resent him or blame him for the way that he was conceived.

His voice was no longer cheerful. Any excitement that may have been felt decimated even faster than the excitement had begun. He asked if he could call me back in an hour to talk with his boyfriend about my proposal.

Ten minutes later, I received a callback. Chance's voice was somber and direct, "Hi, you were the girl that called concerning the baby?"

I replied, "Yes." My heart raced as I waited for an answer. They had to be his parents. I single-handedly chose them because they were perfect.

He inhaled sharply as he said, "Yeah, um, we're going to have to decline. I hope you can understand. With the baby's conception and all, we can't take a risk, besides we're planning on backpacking through Europe in a couple months, and we couldn't possibly take a baby, climbing mountains and all that stuff. We're taking a break from looking to work on ourselves. Thanks so much for your time.

I held back lamented tears as I said, "Thank you. Goodbye."

I hung up the phone as a voice spoke on the other side, but I was holding back a mental breakdown.

My brain was glitching and burning up as I couldn't help but hold my breath until I whispered, "They don't want my baby..."

The words kept repeating until I screamed, "They don't want my baby! They don't want..."

Anger and sorrow filled my mind simultaneously. I was at a loss, feeling rage at my engorged stomach and pity for the unwanted child developing in my body.

Within his voice, it was my story that made him turn away. Who would give up their greatest wish for a vacation? I cried for hours after the call. Since they didn't want him, it felt like nobody ever would. As he turned within me, I felt the little feet press against my stomach, and my hand caressed him in turn.

It had to have been hard for him, too. Living inside a teenager who didn't want to keep him and feeling an unknown loss at every turn with me that I hoped he would no longer feel when he was given his family. Living inside my belly had to have been such a dismal place.

An amazing thing about adoption is that nobody really knows unless you've been through it. There are several different kinds of adoptions. The process that comes to mind when adoption is spoken about is a closed adoption. This is chosen as a completely anonymous option. The new parents' names and locations are unknown, even if you were to ask. The child will only know if they ask the state after they turn eighteen. This is scary for some. The baby may not be wanted, but you may wonder in time how they're doing if they're happy, or what their family looks like. I didn't like the idea of so many unknowns.

An open adoption has more options, even visits in some cases, depending on what options you ask for. There are fewer couples willing to do this, as what they ask for is asked before your wants. It all depends on how comfortable they might feel. Unfortunately, they are never allowed to change their mind. If it doesn't go well, or it confuses the child too much, they have to live with that burden because of a decision they thought they could live with before it occurred. The only way to change it is by a court order. That would be incredibly difficult for all individuals involved if it didn't go in an agreed manner. It's the way that I'm sure adoptees dread, even if not at first. I didn't want that much from the parents. It was their job to be mom and dad. All I wanted to know for as long as I felt I needed to know, was that they were happy. I wanted him to be loved as a human, as any child deserves, and seen as part of their family, if not the center of their universe. Love is the main thing a child needs to be able to grow, live happily, and be better off than I had ever been. The baby was more than me, not less than. It was the evolution from couple to family. I tried to choose with that in mind. With whom would he be most loved?

Mom found a small, local agency and asked me to set up an appointment. I called and was told that I would be allowed the choice of choosing the family for the baby I was carrying. I went through stacks of portfolios of couples twice a week. All of the couples either already had children. I didn't want old parents because how would they play with them? If they already had children and were able to have more, how could this one be seen as anything more than just a pet? He didn't deserve to be the family pet or the odd one out. The chances of that, even if they were logically low to anyone else, seemed astronomically high to me. I felt like that growing up and hadn't even been adopted. If I had, it would've made a lot more sense to me because I could never be a creation of love, instead, just a stray animal allowed in the house to act as a part of the family, or a robot. It's easy to make someone you don't care about a robot or even a slave. Not if I had anything to do with it.

It took me a while to stop at a portfolio of a single African American man. The adoption lady, Tina, said his boyfriend also had a separate file, although she wasn't supposed to disclose that they were a couple. They were perfect together. One man was black, and the other white, and mutually wanted to adopt. It was the perfect combination.

It's strange that a single man could be considered to adopt a baby, but not a gay couple. The ideologies of society are skewed in many, many ways. That was one of them. If two people are in love and want to be a family, it shouldn't matter what gender the pair is. Even if a couple were more than two people. It was all the more love to go around, especially when it comes to loving a child. How could that not be seen? A married couple that wanted a baby to band-aid their marriage would be considered far more easily than a deserving one that didn't agree with the morals of society. Society is far too judgemental of unimportant things that affect no one but the victims of judgment. I wouldn't have chosen a single man because, what if he met a woman and had their own kids together? Where would it leave him? What if he decided to step out? I didn't have the highest opinion of straight men from my experiences in life.

The only thing was that after Tina called them with the good news, they informed her because of how the baby was conceived, it would be difficult putting him first or think of him as a real son. Also, they disclosed that because one of them had a daughter from a previous marriage, she would always be put first. They would never look at him as their real son. It would be difficult to even love him because he was a product of rape. He could do the same when he grew up.

Tina called that night and informed me of what they had said. Although they were still willing to adopt, it would be a bad choice. She was taking them off her adoption list because of what they said. Her agency was called "A Baby to Love," so if that wouldn't be given, there was no point in finding them a baby to treat as second best, if not last.

Tina returned the next week with one last book she was certain I would like. She had been looking through all of her files every day to find one that would be ideal for me. What was interesting about her files was that questions were asked when the couples made their portfolios that included gender, race, and conception preferences and what kind adoption they would like.

The couple she brought to me had been pushed to the back of the files. Money puts you at the top of the pile, even when the want and need of a barren, childless couple is greater. I was looking for quality, not wealth.

The only thing that made me question them was the fact that they were both Caucasian. *How would this baby ever feel like he belonged? How would people look at them and see a family? Society would likely see the mother as a cheater and the dad as a fool for keeping them both. It worried me because the last thing I wanted him to be was resented.*

I spoke with the soon to be Mom on the phone a few days after accepting them as the recipients. She answered all of my questions and relieved all doubts in my mind. This couple didn't care what people might think and would love him unconditionally throughout his life. They had been trying to conceive for years until finding out they were both sterile and would never be able to create a baby on their own. They had been waiting to adopt for five years without a single call to tell them they would be parents.

I gave birth a month later, and his parents met him the same day a few hours afterwards, as their flight had run late, causing them to miss his birth. Besides the medical staff, his real mother, that would be adopting him, was the first person to hold him. She instantly fell in love. The look in her eyes made it certain that she was the one. She looked at him with tears in her eyes and an uncontainable smile on her face, as if she was holding the world in her hands. He was instantly everything that mattered to her. Nothing else mattered.

The medical staff often asked me if I was sure I wanted the adoptive parents in the same room with me and the baby. They kept asking if I wanted to hold him or try to feed him with my breast. They tried to get me to hold him or, at the very least, look at him, but I declined.

I peeked at him once, and tears filled my eyes with warm disgust. I never held him because when I looked at his face, all I could see was my rapist. Looking at him, I even saw the scar that went from his eye to his cheekbone. I trusted he was beautiful by the look on his mother's face when she looked at him. Mom informed me he was perfect and there was no scar, just transference. I would've never been able to keep him, even if I wanted to. I couldn't overcome what had happened to bring him to life, even just to look at him.

All I asked from them was to try to find a brother of the same race as him, so he would never feel different or alone. I asked for pictures for four years of his life to ensure he was happy, remained loved, and developed normally. After three years of loving him, his parents adopted a baby brother with the same heritage. He would never feel alone in any way.

Nurture can defy the nature of any event. My tragedy grew someone that may not have turned into a treasure otherwise. His parents believed every child is born innocent, which I learned was a rare mindset. But it made all the difference. They were a beautiful growing family, and I couldn't have made a better choice.
Out of a nightmare,
I created love.

20. Tranquility

 I walked down the stairs of the apartment into the snowy night. I didn't think of the darkness. I didn't fear the shadow. I only thought about the glacial breeze caressing my skin and the velvety fabric of my suede jacket pressing against my skin.

 I looked out at the clouds of snow covering the tops of cars, roofs, and land all around. The painted parking lot felt abandoned, yet more peaceful than it had ever been before. I turned towards the snow-capped bushes at the branches swaddled in ice. Underneath a nearby shrub laid a bony mound of brown and tan fur. Had an animal froze to death? It was far too frigid to be unprotected in a blanket made of snow.

 I bent down to take a closer look at the frozen creature, only to see a set of hazel eyes blinking back at me. A gentle motor played the most soothing sounds in the body of the frozen beauty. She shivered in the snow as she stood up to greet me, moving slowly from the chill just to rub against my leg to say a proper hello. Her whiskers were icicles; her fur was made of bones. I picked her up from the ground and tucked her into my jacket for warmth. She didn't fight. She only purred louder as she was swaddled in warmth. I examined her closely as she lay curled inside my jacket, pressed against my pregnant belly that was growing life. She seemed to be smiling with her whiskers pointing out in a circle as her lips grew further apart. She still had so much beauty and was strong enough to stay alive in the winter freeze.

I wasn't sure if I would be allowed to keep her, but she looked just like Leo, only thinner. She had to have a survivor's spirit being out in the freezing snow. I needed something to help me feel safe; she was my gift from the answering universe. She needed me to save her life, and I needed a reason to live.

She slept under the blankets with me every night, even when she wasn't cold. I was her safe place, and she was mine. I never wanted to be anywhere but near her.

I thought of the day I met my beautiful cat, Staind, as I laid in bed at the motel in Texas. I couldn't help but stare at her before I fell asleep as she curled up under the blankets with me. She was my best friend in the entire world because we saved each other the day I found her in the snow. I could talk to her anytime, and she would stare at me and seem to listen. I could cry into her ribs, and all she would do is stay still and purr. She was my happy place, a reason to move on.

I didn't like leaving the house because that would mean I would have to leave her too. I had a bit of an extreme attachment to her. Mom explained it was because my natural mother instincts kicked in, and she was my baby to love in place of the one I gave away.

My socializing was done on a computer screen on numerous websites and instant messengers, and that's all I needed for any type of attention besides attention from her. I was a teenager, after all, so part of me needed to be somewhere in the world. I traveled everywhere in my mind. I learned all I needed from books I wished to study. I read encyclopedias, textbooks, and literary fiction that explored imaginary worlds and kingdoms, all with Staind in my lap.

I finally felt at peace. Tranquil even. I never wanted anything more.

Everyone has the capability of being whole, regardless of what has been done to you or what has happened in your life. However broken you feel, try to learn to love all of your broken shards and find a way to glue them together, even if they're bound to break again. It's a tiring process, I know. Sometimes, the puzzle bursts before you even have the chance to begin. It feels hopeless trying to constantly rebuild yourself. It never comes out the same way because pieces have multiplied, and others go missing. All that matters is that you try as often as possible to find the light at the end of the tunnel. Each end is where a new beginning starts again.

Happiness can be the most difficult thing to find, especially after the world has given you pain, torment, neglect, and so much more that is impossible to bear. Take a deep breath. I can't promise it'll be better,, but the light will eventually shine through. Try with all your might to find a way through. Believe in yourself like it's the only thing keeping the air in your lungs. Mute the inner demons that try to tear you apart with more positive thoughts. There is something good about every single person. Even the worst human in the world has to have one good quality, even if everything else is bad. Find out what yours is, and once you do, remind yourself daily of that. Find something else and add it to your list until you have all the reasons to love yourself, even if you feel like nobody else does or ever could.

I know how that feels. I know what it's like to be betrayed and thrown away. It doesn't make you anything less than anyone else. People can walk over you every day, which does not make them better than you. It does not make you less. It makes them cruel, but not superior. Wealth does not make you king of the world, nor does poverty put you to the bottom. Society would like for you to think it does, but nothing matters at all except your inner peace and love for yourself.

What the world needs is more love, the best place to start is to see it in yourself, to show kindness to others that seem to be having a worse day than you. Find your bliss and go with it.

Even if you fail, try, try again, and you will be a success. Claw yourself out from the bottom until it's no longer an obstacle to climb.

I make it sound simple, but I know that it's not. I have only felt love for myself and inner peace for brief periods of time throughout my life. When you forget how to breathe, your body starts suffocating.

But, what doesn't kill you only makes you more interesting.

Never let the monsters win.

Made in the USA
Coppell, TX
25 January 2025

44034131R00115